DESTINATION: EXCELLENCE

THE JOURNEY OF SKYWEST AIRLINES

BY COLLEEN BIRCH MAILE

PUBLISHED BY GO! PUBLICATIONS, INC.
205 NORTH 10TH STREET, SUITE M-1
BOISE, IDAHO 83702
208-333-9990

Publisher KELLY D. COLES
Art Director KRISTINA MITCHELL
Graphic Designer LESLIE SASSO
Copy Editor JEANETTE GERMAIN
Achievement Profiles by DIANE RONAYNE

© 2002, All Rights Reserved, Published 2002
Printed in USA, First Edition
ISBN 0-9726101-0-3

THIS BOOK IS DEDICATED TO

ALL THE EMPLOYEES OF SKYWEST AIRLINES—

PAST, PRESENT AND FUTURE, AND

TO EVERYONE WHO BELIEVES THAT IN AMERICA

ANYTHING IS POSSIBLE.

ACKNOWLEDGEMENTS

Thanks are in order to everyone who made this book a reality.
I am especially grateful to SkyWest Airlines "family" members willing
to share stories and mementos of the past. These include
Jerry Atkin, Ron Reber, Ralph and Cheri Atkin, Sid Atkin,
Klen Brooks, Eric Christensen and Steve Hart.

Special recognition must be given to the insight, vision and irrepressible
energy of SkyWest's People Department Director Alison Gemmell. She
sparked this project and made its completion possible. The able assistance
of Communications Manager Sabrena Suite also proved invaluable.

— *Colleen Birch Maile*

CONTENTS

With each **twist and turn,** opportunity & challenge

SkyWest adapted without sacrificing principles.

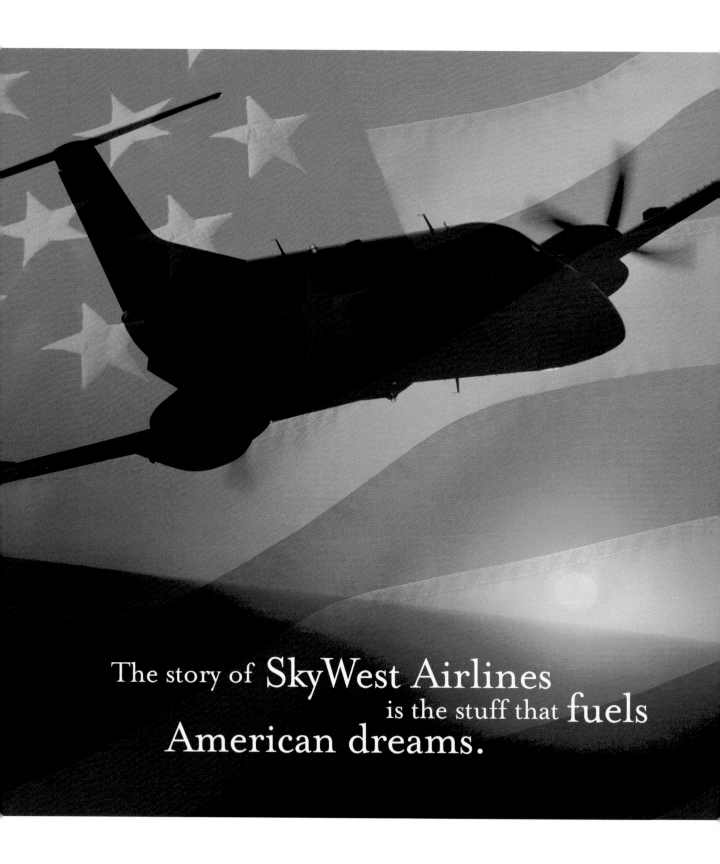

The story of SkyWest Airlines is the stuff that fuels American dreams.

A CHRONICLE OF PERSEVERANCE

In 1972, the world was a wider place. No supersonic transports linked the globe. Computers required a room of their own. "Out of the way" described much of America's most spectacular landscape.

That year, in tiny St. George, Utah, Sky-West Airlines began with three part-time pilots and four planes — none of them pressurized or air-conditioned. The top craft in the fleet boasted six-seats.

There was no grand mission statement, no elaborate business plan, just a group of friends determined to do something about the lack of regular air service to their little town. The one aim — to shuttle passengers between the mesa of St. George, a nearby mountain town, Cedar City, and the state capital in Salt Lake. The founders vowed to stick to a schedule — no matter what. They've kept their word and then some.

In 2002, SkyWest Airlines marked 30 years of achievement. During the company's first three decades, mankind experienced unparalleled progress. Technology evolved to carry information and ideas across geographic barriers at ever-increasing speeds. Advancements in transportation made it possible to quickly transcend time zones. Once remote areas turned into highly sought leisure destinations and business locations. A product of its place in time, SkyWest Airlines, operating continuously from St. George, Utah, grew to become America's largest independent regional airline, serving as both a Delta Connection and United Express carrier. In 2002, the company provided approximately 1,000 daily flights to 83 cities in 23 Western states and Canada. It carried more than half a million people each month — quite the increase from the 256 passengers accommodated during its first year.

That level of growth and success is remarkable in any industry. The accomplishment is particularly noteworthy given the tenuous nature of regional aviation. Most of the "short-haul" air carriers in existence when SkyWest first took to the skies were long gone by 2002. The story of SkyWest's stellar survival is the stuff that fuels American dreams.

Closer examination reveals that this saga isn't about business people determined to grow a company no matter the cost. Instead, it is a chronicle of small decisions — choices grounded in the determination to do the right thing. These seemingly inconsequential day-to-day events amounted to huge results for SkyWest and those it serves.

It's a story worth telling. Even so, this book is more than just the tale of one company. It is also an account of an industry in the throes of change — from deregulation to code sharing, from teletype machines to computerized reservation systems, from the crowded runways and bustling concourses of the 1990s to the stifling silence of airports vacated for four days in September, 2001.

With each twist and turn, opportunity and challenge, SkyWest adapted without sacrificing principles. Its legacy of achievement establishes that it is possible for an American business to be both profitable and honorable. That is a lesson that will stand the test of time.

The 1972 cornerstone — *seeing a need* and

NINE-SEAT PIPER NAVAJO
FLYING OVER LAKE POWELL, UTAH

diligently **working to fill it**

1972 to 1981
THE SURVIVAL YEARS

Seeing a need and working to fill it — that simple, yet powerful concept is the cornerstone of SkyWest Airlines. In the 1960s and 1970s, remote St. George, Utah seemed like a place with ample demand for air service. As the gateway to Zion and Bryce National Parks, the southern Utah town enjoyed a brisk tourist trade. It was also home to Dixie College, site of an Aerotech program. Plenty of pilots, mechanics and aviation buffs lived in the area. In the decades after World War II, dozens of air service companies were attracted to St. George. They ranged from one-man local charters to well-respected commercial carriers. None lasted very long.

In those days, the federal government's Civil Aeronautics Board (CAB) mandated service to many smaller American destinations. Although St. George had an airport, the CAB subsidy for service went to Cedar City — 50 miles away via a two-lane highway. Many St. George citizens preferred to fly to Cedar City, Salt Lake City and points beyond. However, sometimes they'd book a flight, get to the airport and wait for a plane that didn't come. The air carriers, when confronted with a skimpy St. George manifest, would decide that landing at the city's airfield wasn't worth the time. The plane would fly on to Cedar City, while would-be travelers craned their necks on the St. George tarmac.

The shoddy service was especially frustrating for St. George's business community. In 1972, Dixie Airlines, the city's one remaining provider, was about to close shop. Ralph Atkin, a young attorney and budding pilot, decided something had to be done. He gathered four friends, formed a corporation, and sold shares with the intent of starting a passenger service to Salt Lake City. It was rough going. By the first board meeting, three of the five organizers had lost interest. Ralph Atkin and Jerry Fackrell, director of the College's Aerotech program, installed themselves and their wives as officers, bought back the other men's shares and on April 26, 1972 purchased the Dixie Airlines' operating certificate and a 10-year airport lease.

Two weeks later, the newly named SkyWest Airlines invited all of St. George to tour their meager, concrete block "office" and take airplane rides priced according to passenger weight at a penny per pound. There were four craft in the SkyWest fleet—a Piper Seneca and Cherokee Six, each boasting six seats, plus a two-seat Piper Cherokee and a four-seat Cherokee Arrow.

When Jerry Fackrell piloted the first official flight to Salt Lake on June 19, the round trip from St. George to Salt Lake City cost $59. Passengers traveling from Cedar City to Salt Lake got an $8 discount. Regular flights were scheduled for Mondays, Wednesdays and Fridays. To win public confidence, planes flew even if there were no passengers. Two months later, $30 was slashed off the price to draw more business. As expected, demand for SkyWest service increased. Profits, however, remained elusive. In October, Fackrell left the company. Earl Snow, the only remaining pilot, went to work full time for less than $60 a week.

Ralph Atkin recruited more friends and family members including his brother, Sid,

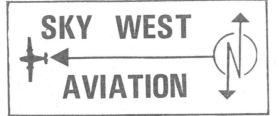

As this early newspaper ad depicts, in 1972, pilots and passengers became well acquainted while flying the "spacious" six-seat Seneca.

proprietor of St. George's Sugar Loaf Café and a state legislator. Determined to do whatever it took to fly the SkyWest schedule, they diversified — operating a flight school and a fixed-base operation (FBO), seeding clouds for farmers, and transporting illegal aliens to deportation centers on behalf of the federal government. They ran "flightseeing" tours and added service to Las Vegas. Despite all the effort, the young company soon confronted mountainous debt.

Enter the Atkins' 25-year-old nephew. Armed with a CPA license, an MBA degree and an entrepreneurial spirit, Jerry Atkin was willing to lend a hand. The only objective — SkyWest's survival.

The young accountant spent his first year on the job warding off creditors while Ralph and Sid tried to sell the airline for $25,000. No one was interested. They attempted to give SkyWest away. No takers. The Atkins knew they should declare bankruptcy. But the descendants of stoic St. George pioneers refused.

Instead they sold aircraft, cut staff, modified routes and crafted a creative payback plan. Creditors cooperated. Family members anteed up for more stock. The State of Utah did its part awarding the company $15,000 in grant money aimed at encouraging tourism. In the midst of the reorganization Jerry Atkin became the youngest president of a regularly scheduled airline — ever. He was 26 years old.

There was no glamour in the position. Like all early SkyWest employees, Jerry Atkin became a master of flexibility. He loaded bags, pumped gas, boarded passengers, and shared a drafty, spider-infested workspace in SkyWest "headquarters" — a windowless tin hangar. He priced tickets, crunched numbers and stretched cash. By the third quarter of 1976, the company showed a tiny profit. Within a year, all the obligations were met.

The turn of fortune came just as the federal government decided to "deregulate" airlines. Market factors, not government mandates, would determine which carriers provided service to a community. The airline willing to serve small, subsidized communities would continue to receive payments for 10 years. SkyWest became one of three regional airlines certified by the Civil Aeronautics Board, and when it replaced Hughes AirWest at Cedar City, Utah, and Page, Arizona its service was subsidized. That infusion of regular revenue funded a new $500,000 office/hangar complex and the purchase of a 19-seat Metroliner, a pressurized turbo-prop known for comfort and reliability.

As the larger airlines, beleaguered by rising fuel costs, abandoned the small cities and towns, SkyWest was primed to fill the gap — so were other, more established regional carriers.

Ron Reber, who started as a counter agent in Cedar City, led SkyWest's foray into Pocatello, Idaho. Following the lead of competitors — Cascade, Mountain West and TransWestern — Ron called on travel agents. His promotional tool — SkyWest's flight schedule, hand-scrawled on orange construction paper. It included the phone number in St. George — SkyWest's only booking method. The travel agents gently explained that all the other airlines took part in a computerized reservation system (CRS). That piece of information opened a whole new world for the little airline from Utah. As it sought to become a CRS participant, its reputation for reliability and customer service earned it an increased market share.

When the aviation industry was hit hard by the air traffic controller's strike of 1981, SkyWest was one of only five American airlines to show a profit. Despite unsettling times for many other airlines, at the end of its tenth year, SkyWest was ready to grow. ✈

> As the larger airlines beleagured by rising fuel costs abandoned small cities and towns, SkyWest was primed to fill the gap.

We give you Salt Lake City

3 times a day

Now we've made it easier than ever before to fly to Salt Lake City — three flights daily! Leave St. George on our 7:00 a.m. flight, arrive in Salt Lake before 9:00 a.m. You'll have an entire working day in the city and still be home in time for dinner. (Our evening flight departs Salt Lake at 5:45 p.m.)

Catch our handy 2:50 p.m. or 5:35 p.m. flights for an evening in Salt Lake. Stay overnight and return on the 7:00 a.m. flight the next morning. You'll be home in time for breakfast. Now that's convenience!

Find out about our other convenient flights — pick up our new expanded flight schedule at our reservation desk in the Four Seasons Office Plaza.

Salt Lake three times a day — and we're still growing strong!

This 1974 ad did little to improve SkyWest's fortunes. In 1975, flights to Provo, Utah, were dropped and Moab and Bullfrog, Utah, were served only seasonally. By decade's end, all three destinations were gone but SkyWest added larger markets – Pocatello, Idaho, and Phoenix and Flagstaff, Arizona.

SkyWest's first flight on June 19, 1972 captured the local newspaper's attention. Piper Aircraft representative Larry Mendenall gave the keys to SkyWest's first Piper Seneca to Chairman Ralph Atkin, who is accompanied by SkyWest General Manager Jerry Fackrell, on his right.

From left to right: Larry Mendenhall, Don Wittkie, Ralph Atkin, Jerry Fackrell, Bill Thomas and Bob Farley. Larry Mendenhall hands keys of new "72" Seneca to Ralph Atkin.

New Air Service Opens In Dixie

Jerry Fackrell and Ralph Atkin are the new owners of the St. George airport. According to Mr. Atkin the airport name will be changed to "Sky West Aviation Incorporated." Mr. Fackrell will be the General Manager and Mr. Atkin will serve as president of the corporation.

The new airport will offer total flight service including flight instruction, private and commercial flights, instruction ratings, multi-engine ratings, instrument ratings, and complete maintenance service. "We will offer charter service to anywhere in the continental United States for families or groups," stated Mr. Atkin.

Beginning June 19, Sky West will have commuter flights to Salt Lake City on a five day a week basis. Flights to Las Vegas will also be available. The flights will be made in a 1972 model, twin-engine Seneca.

Mr. Atkin also reported that the airport has acquired two new planes. They have three trained pilots who are skilled mechanics as well as flight instructors.

Sky West Aviation Incorporated will be an authorized Piper dealer for the entire Southern Utah area. Mr. Atkin says, "We are offering the finest flight service in all of Southern Utah."

kh

The Piper Navajo, added to SkyWest's fleet in 1974, was a piston-engine plane designed for eight passengers and two pilots. However, SkyWest typically used it as a nine-passenger plane affording much inter-action between pilot and passengers.

FAST FACTS:

After WWII, an ample supply of inexpensive planes and seasoned pilots spawned dozens of airlines. At one time or another, Challenger, West, Bonanza, Air West and Dixie Airlines served St. George, Utah.

1972

First regular board meeting March 2

First flight June 19

1973

St. George population: 10,000

Dixie Airlines certificate and airport lease purchased in April

Dean Christensen, Frank Allen, Harold Chesler, Mervyn K. Cox, joined the board.

This concrete terminal building housed SkyWest's early operations. Alan Olson (pictured at left) served as co-pilot of the inaugural flight.

SkyWest founder, Ralph Atkin, at the control of a Piper Navajo with wife, Cheri, the company's original secretary, in the right seat, and their children Launale, 5, and Shanna, 18 months.

SkyWest's three original pilots, Jerry Fackrell, Paul Leddy and Earl Snow (pictured above) were paid $5 an hour for flight time only. When Snow became the first full time employee, his weekly salary totaled $59.72.

" We never had much trouble with **maintenance** because we did a lot of preventative things. We really researched the 'what-ifs?'. **"**

– EARL SNOW,
PILOT AND FORMER
MAINTENANCE DIRECTOR

FAST FACTS:
During SkyWest's "do-it-yourself" bankruptcy, its greatest creditor, Hughes Aviation, was owed $5,000. Impressed by the straightforward honesty of the SkyWest team, Hughes agreed to a year's worth of $50 monthly payments and a renegotiated payback schedule. The parties signed a handwritten agreement and shook hands on it.

Financial system established in April; board expanded to seven members; new stockholders infused $40,000

1974

Acquired first
Navajo Chieftain

Acceptance in Aviation Clearing House enabled
SkyWest to write tickets on other airlines.

"When people don't want what you offer, stick with it,

Come to SKYWEST'S OPEN HOUSE

It's All Happening At The Airport!

★ Acrobatic air show   ★ Guided Tours
★ $5⁰⁰ airplane rides   ★ Airplane Displays
★ FREE Refreshments
★ FUN FOR THE WHOLE FAMILY

Saturday, May 2, 9 A.M. to 5 P.M.

See

LEARN TO FLY
With The Professional Pilots Of
SKYWEST AIRLINES

THAT'S RIGHT! NOW YOU CAN OBTAIN YOUR FLIGHT INSTRUCTION FROM THE PROFESSIONAL PILOTS OF SKYWEST AIRLINES. THEY'LL TEACH YOU ALL THE NECESSARY PILOT SKILLS TO BECOME A REALLY SAFE PRIVATE PILOT. YOU'LL LEARN IN MODERN AIRCRAFT ESPECIALLY DESIGNED BY CESSNA AND GRUMMAN AMERICAN. SO DON'T DEBATE ANY LONGER — COME FLY WITH THE "THE PROFESSIONALS."

Fly To Manti
for the
"Mormon Miracle Pageant"
July 10, 11, 12, 15-19, 1975

SKYWEST AIRLINES IS OFFERING SPECIAL CHARTER FLIGHTS FROM ST. GEORGE AND CEDAR CITY TO THE "MORMON MIRACLE PAGEANT" IN MANTI, UTAH. ROUND TRIP CHARTER RATES ARE (INCLUDING GROUND TRANSPORTATION TO AND FROM THE MANTI AIRPORT):

ONLY $39 per person

FLY DIXIE AIRLINES

N8920N

FABULOUS SCENIC TOURS

THE GRAND CANYON TOUR
(3 HOURS ROUND TRIP)

THE SCENIC PARKS TOUR
(4 HOURS ROUND TRIP)

"The Sleek
Birds with
the Proud
Tails"

DIXIE AIRLINES

SKY WEST AIRLINES TAKES YOU TO "AMERICA'S COLOR CANYONS"

ZION NATIONAL PARK

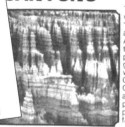

BRYCE CANYON

The newest and most exciting vacation concept for seeing "America's Color Canyons" is now available through SkyWest Airlines. This concept is the air-tour! Your professional airline pilot becomes your airborne tour guide as he shows you the wonders of Zion's National Park, Cedar Breaks, Bryce Canyon, or Grand Canyon. From your armchair in the sky, you can photograph scenes that will be prized mementoes of your fantastic aerial excursion.

Zion, Cedar Breaks, Snow's Canyon	* $29.00
Bryce Canyon	* $42.00
Grand Canyon	** $42.00

ALL FLIGHTS DEPART FROM ST. GEORGE AIRPORT

FOR SCENIC FLIGHT AIR-TOUR INFORMATION CALL:
ST. GEORGE AREA 673-6101 | OTHER UTAH CITIES (800)662-4237 TOLL FREE | OUTSIDE UTAH (800)453-9117 TOLL FREE

Yes! Please send me my FREE copy of Sky West Airlines Award Winning Brochure. "America's Color Canyons"

NAME

ADDRESS

CITY _____ STATE _____ ZIP _____

(MAIL YOUR REQUEST TO: SKY WEST AIRLINES, BOX T, ST. GEORGE, UTAH 84770.)

For SkyWest marketers

do your best and you'll change their minds."

Finally... an Airline of your very own.

SKY WEST AIRLINES now offers daily flights to Cedar City, St. George and Las Vegas right from the Provo Airport. In the same time it used to take just to drive to the Salt Lake Airport you can now be arriving in Cedar City. That's important to the busy commuter. Call us and we'll send you the complete flight schedule.

We're yours...Use us!

SKY WEST AIRLINES INFORMATION 801/377 7720 RESERVATION

LET IT SNOW!

Yes, let it snow! SkyWest's radar equipped aircraft are completely prepared for operations under winter instrument conditions. We fly to Salt Lake City, Cedar City, St. George, and Las Vegas three times a day. We also fly everyday to Provo, Utah and Page, Arizona. Don't take a chance driving on icy roads, have SkyWest

RESERVATIONS 800/662-4237 TOLL FREE
INFORMATION 801/673-6101

THE MOST FLIGHTS AND LOWEST FARES TO SOUTHERN UTAH

This Winter when the uncrowded, deep powder of Brian Head, or the sun-drenched golf courses of St. George draw you to Color Country, remember Sky West gives you the best service there.

Sky West has the most flights to Cedar City and the only flights to St. George. That saves you a costly car rental and a long time-wasting drive.

And since Sky West has the lowest fares to both cities, you

actually save enough on a round-trip flight to pay for a first-class dinner and show.

But we also want you to know how great our schedules are. Write or send your business card to: Sky West Airlines. St. George Municipal Airport. St. George. Utah 84770. We'll send you our handy flight schedule. Or call toll free. 800-622-4237 for reservations.

Sky West Airlines. We give you executive service, at bargain prices.

We make it FUN to fly!

SKY WEST AIRLINES DAILY COMMUTER

- Commuter Service
- Scenic Flights
- Charter Service
- Air Ambulance
- Aircraft Maintenance
- Flight Instruction
- Air freight
- Rentals
- Air Taxi

ST. GEORGE AIRPORT	CEDAR CITY AIRPORT
673-6101	**586-3033**

Toll Free Reservations **800-662-4237**

persistence paid off.

Early employees who played critical roles in the company's development included (l to r) Earl Snow, John Ligtermoet, Alan Olson, Jerry Allredge, Klen Brooks, and Val Williams (not pictured).

FAST FACTS: SkyWest's 1974 acceptance in the Airline Clearing House cooperative meant that it was able to book and write tickets on airlines traveling to destinations beyond Salt Lake City.

As majority whip of the Utah Legislature, Sid Atkin, SkyWest board member, made a plea to enhance air service to rural Utah.

1975

Efforts to sell or give away the airline failed.

Jerry Atkin became youngest president of an airline at age 26. Ralph Atkin goes back to practice law.

1976

First profitable year, launched 12-year profitability streak.

"Creative Payback" program conquered debt.

SkyWest's seven-aircraft fleet outside the airline's original terminal building at St. George Municipal Airport.

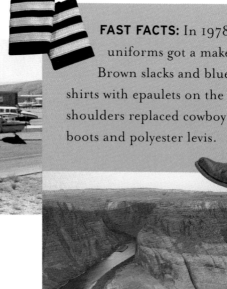

FAST FACTS: In 1978, pilots' uniforms got a makeover. Brown slacks and blue shirts with epaulets on the shoulders replaced cowboy boots and polyester levis.

Ron Reber, Chief Executive Officer, shown in 1978 with Kelly Mumford, who became Director of Customer Relations. He began his SkyWest career as a Cedar City counter agent when the station's furnishings consisted of a board across two boxes and a beat up couch.

In 1978, SkyWest replaced Hughes Aircraft at Cedar City, Utah and Page, Arizona and made Page a routing lynchpin linking Salt Lake City, Las Vegas and Phoenix. Pictured above: Horseshoe Bend of the Colorado River, south of Page, Arizona.

After deregulation in 1978, SkyWest's arrival in a community typically meant a larger carrier was leaving. "We were never greeted with open arms. In fact we were somewhat held in contempt. It was always an uphill battle to win those people over. But there's something to be said for the underdog position. You have everything to win and nothing to lose. Our troops always rallied. We lost a few battles, but I'd say we won every war."
— RON REBER, CHIEF EXECUTIVE OFFICER

1977

1978

SkyWest was third commuter airline to become a regularly certified air carrier operating with the same responsibilities and regulations as major airlines.

Interline agreement with American, Hughes, United and Texas International Airlines expedited check-in and baggage ticketing.

In 1978, SkyWest Airlines was transformed by

the Fairchild Metroliner.

FAIRCHILD METROLINER FLYING
THROUGH ZION NATIONAL PARK, UTAH

The first Metroliner cost $1.4 million. Its purchase was made possible by "ultra-fast" financing arranged in less than a week by Duane Grobman of McDonnell Douglas Finance Corporation, shown at right with Jerry Atkin.

The Metro's first flight July, 1979. (l to r) Lee Murdoch of Murdoch Travel, Airport Director Paul Gaines, Rudger Atkin, Sid Atkin, Eldon Tanner, Utah Governor Scott Matheson, Jerry Atkin, Ralph Atkin, St. George Mayor Grey Larkin

FAST FACTS: At the start of 1979, SkyWest's fleet consisted of five Navajo Chieftains. That year, the airline made a significant addition to the fleet. It purchased a 19-passenger Metroliner, the first aircraft designed expressly for regional use. Powered by a turbine engine, the pressurized and air-conditioned Metroliner transformed the little airline.

1978

Deregulation – October 24 – single most important factor in survival of small community air service

Civil Aeronautics Board approved three-year annual subsidy of $160,000 for Metroliner service to Page, Arizona and $145,000 to Cedar City, Utah.

1979

First 19-seat Metroliner ordered and delivered

SKYWEST AIRLINES

Sue Esplin (left) Michelle Dennis (center) and Valerie Jacobsen (right) at the airline's ticket counter housed with the executive offices at St. George's Four Seasons Convention Center.

Among SkyWest's first innovations— an upgrade in its reservations system that consisted of replacing a blue three ring binder with a modified recipe card box. Situated on a "lazy-Susan" revolving tray, the card box could be easily accessed by several reservationists. John Ligtermoet created the contraption. "I think it took John about a day from the time we came up with the idea. That's the way our people have always worked. When they see something that needs doing, they do it without delay," Jerry Atkin explained.

In 1979, this $500,000 hangar/office building replaced the original corrugated tin headquarters.

> " Navajos were a one-pilot operation: passengers sat in the co-pilot seat and we got to know them real well. That went away with the Metroliners. "
>
> – KLEN BROOKS, PILOT

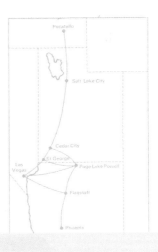

A new hangar opened to house the first Metroliner and others on order.

1980

Service to Pocatello, Idaho, carried SkyWest north.

Increase in fuel prices caused major airlines to abandon markets to the benefit of regional carriers.

ation for the City of St. George

ST. GEORGE, UTAH 84770, THURSDAY, JUNE 22, 1972

New Commuter Air Service Started Here

Sky West Aviation commuter service

Airwest to End Service To Cedar City, Page

Special to The Tribune

CEDAR CITY — Cedar City officials have ivil Aeronautics Board that Hughes Airwest has been authorized to suspend air service at Cedar City and Page, Ariz., for a period of three years.

Hughes Airwest, which presently serves both cities on a regular run between Salt Lake City and Las Vegas, Nev., had petitioned the board last year for suspension and deletion of service.

Hearings were held in Cedar City by Administrative Law Judge William A. Kane Jr. last summer. Following those hearings Judge Kane recommended to the CAB that Airwest's authority to service Cedar City and Page should not be deleted or unconditionally suspended.

CAB Suspension

The current CAB suspension ruling carries several conditions. These include requirements that the suspension order would terminate within 30 days if Sky West Aviation, St. George, (or an acceptable commuter service line) ceased or failed to provide at least two daily round trips Monday through Friday and one round trip on both Saturday and Sunday between Cedar City and either Salt Lake City and Las Vegas; and two daily round trips Monday through Friday and one round trip per weekend between Page and either Salt Lake City or Las Vegas.

Sky West Aviation, a commuter carrier, now makes regular runs on the same route served by Airwest.

Judge Kane, in his initial recommendation, concluded that both Sky West and Cochise (another carrier currently serving Page) would not be able to serve Cedar City or Page for a very long period without some form of subsidy.

Joint Tariffs

Airwest will also be required to maintain all joint tariffs now in effect. Sky West will have to concur in its local passenger fares and cargo rates to and from Cedar City and Page, and these rates cannot exceed rates which Airwest would charge if it were serving Cedar City with its own aircraft.

The CAB ruling states that "our review of the record leads us to conclude that the future need for local air service at these small communities can most successfully be met by reliable, small aircraft service."

The ruling also cited a saving in federal tax dollars. Annual subsidy needed for the continuation of Airwest's pattern of service to the two cities was estimated at nearly $480,000 or more than $58 per passenger.

Mayor Kerry Jones of Cedar City h called a special council meeting bef Monday morning to consider pos appeals to the ruling.

Sky West Airlines ys 30,000

West Airlines , Jerry Atkin, presented a n award to Mr. Jeff the 30,000th flown by Sky West Mr. Frehner was d a special gold

expressed strong suppor the commuter air se offered to Southern Uta Sky West, a Southern based commuter airline. airline offers three r trips daily from St. George and Cedar City to Salt Lake

SKY WEST AIRLINE GIVES AWARD- Jerry Atkin, President of Sky West presents Gold plaque to Jeff Frehner for being the 30,000th passenger to fly the airline.

Skywest sets record in April

ST. GEORGE--SkyWest Airlines set another record in the month of April for passengers served in the Salt Lake City/southern Utah market. SkyWest carried 1,098 passengers between Salt Lake City, Cedar City and St. George in the month of April.

The previous record was set in March with 1,030 passengers. Total passengers served in the month of April tallied 1,467. This is a 25 per cent increase from the prior year.

The increase is attributed to the additional flight initiated in March beginning the fifth year of business for SkyWest.

...kywest, headquartered in their own hangar and office complex at the St. George airport, is one of the areas largest employers, providing jobs for more than 190 people. The airline has chalked up solid growth over the past several years, and promises to grow even further in the future.

Add 50 employees

Skywest continues growth while other airlines cut back

by Gail Thueson
Staff Writer

ST. GEORGE — Despite a national economy that has bounced along like an overloaded cargo plane trying to take off, the largest aviation firm in southern Utah has managed some surprising growth over the past year.

While other airlines have cut back on services, dropped some less than lucrative flights, and laid off employees, St. George based Skywest Airlines has managed to add several new cities, buy new planes, and create jobs for more than 50 additional people.

"It's been a good year for us," says Jerry Atking, company president. "We've had our problems with high interest rates and higher costs, but all in all, we're very happy with Skywest's growth over the past year.

That happiness is due in part to the recent addition of five new cities to the list of those serviced by the airline. Those cities are Vernal, Utah; Rock Springs, Wyo., and Ely, Elko and Reno, Nev.

Skywest began flights into and out of Vernal and Rock Springs on March 1 of this year, taking over for Frontier Airlines, which had been servicing the cities.

Flights into the three Nevada cities, which began April 1, previously been serviced by United Airlines.

Skywest was able to begin service to the five new cities in part, because of the Airline Deregulation Act of 1978. Prior to that time, carriers were pretty well tied to servicing a community once they began scheduled flights into that city, even if the routes never showed a profit. With the deregulation act, carriers could freed themselves from unprofitable routes if they could interest another carrier in servicing them. This has proved a boon to both the larger carriers, the majority of whom had at least a few unprofitable routes, and also the smaller regional airlines who were hungry for these cities where they, with smaller planes and less overhead, could operate at a profit.

For Skywest this has been a boon, and part key to its growth. Under these conditions, Skywest was able to take over service to Flagstaff, Ariz., from Frontier Airlines in 1979; Pocatello, Idaho gained in 1980 from Western Airlines, and five cities were added this year from Frontier and Western Airlines. Several other cities could, and probably will, be added to the Skywest list in the future.

To service this ever-growing company, Skywest has had to purchase additional aircraft. To service the five newest acquisitions, Skywest has added new Metroliners to their stable of planes, bringing to five the number of Metroliners the firm now...

An added boon to the local economy is the quality of the firm to service all of their planes in St. George, resulting in several spinoff companies making their headquarters in the city also.

Skywest reaches 100,000 mark

Sky West boarded its 100,000th passenger today.

Mr. Hal K. Whiting of McCord Air Force Base in Washington, was number 100,000. He was visiting his family in St. George and returning to Washington via Sky West from St. George to Las Vegas. This is 100,000 passengers carried in Scheduled service since Sky West's inception in 1972. The 50,000 mark was reached just less than two years ago.

A press conference held at the St. George Airport for the 100,000 celebration also announced new service to Phoenix to begin July 1, 1979, as well as addition of 19 passenger aircraft in selected Sky West flights beginning the same date.

100,000 PASSENGER— Last week turned out to be a happy one for Airman Hal Whiting of the U.S. Air Force who was home on leave with his folks, Mr. and Mrs. George Whiting. It turned out to be a happy one for Sky West Airlines as well. Hal became theri 100,000 paying passenger on his way to report back to his base. He chating withSky West President, Jerry Atkin while Operations Director Earle Snow looks on.

Skywest Airlines is flying high

ST. GEORGE — Skywest is flying high. It is also flying farther from home, more routes, and boarding more ...One of the things this means to St. George is a...

The expansion and success of Skywest along with increased business in the private aviation sector has placed the focus directly on airport needs for the future. The lack of available funds is certainly part of the long range problem.

...of struggle and success furnishes the ...getting available...

Arizona. It is a growing one and one which coul... more with St. George being the northwest, and... terminal of a nationally important system.

The tie between Las Vegas, St. George, and Cedar... just as important and could easily become more s... MX system moves ahead.

The feeder route from Salt Lake City north to Po... ...s is just that according to Atkin. Skywest Pr... ...grow to include Twin Fa... ...low," he comment... ...ve for Idaho." ...ivity at the airport... ...ccording to those ... ...ganization of a air... ...a master plan are ... ...value at the prese... ...ast group who wo...

Utah Commuter Airlines Finally Over the Hump, Economically

, June 18, 1978

By Robert H. Woody
Tribune Business Editor

You don't get a your choice of coffee, tea or milk.

However, air sickness bags are readily on hand. For the hot afternoon summer air can get just a bit choppy.

These are the commuter air...

nine passengers at nine cruising speeds of 230 miles an hour or so.

Trans Western, the smallest of the commuters, employs about 30.

St. George Airline

Utah's second-largest commuter carrier is the St. George-based Sky West Airlines, whose workhorses are also the Navajo Chieftains.

Sky West, like Trans Western, also is owned by a dozen or so investors, principally from southern Utah. It employs 55.

During the present fiscal year, it expects to carry 30,000 passengers with expectation of earning $100,000 on sales of $1,750,000, he said.

The Salt Lake City-based Key Airlines is the biggest, employing 130.

It also has the largest craft — 44-passenger Convair 440s.

It flies between Salt Lake City, Burley, Twin Falls, Boise with a link to Hailey — gateway to Sun Valley.

It will carry 50,000 passengers this year, according to Brent Wiseman,

months by utility rate hearings — has not been considered to be burdensome.

Commuter routes across state lines — provided the craft carries no more than 30 — are exempt from CAB regulation. Key has a variance for its 44-passenger Convairs.

Present deregulation legislation — now approved by committees in the Senate and House — would hike that limitation to 55 passengers.

That, according to Mr. Wiseman, will considerably increase the reach and ...

DESTINATIONS

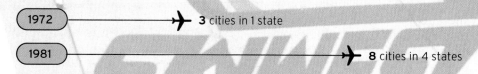

1972 ✈ **3** cities in 1 state

1981 ✈ **8** cities in 4 states

PLANES

1972 ✈ **4**

1981 ✈ **8** – 5 Najavos and 3 Metroliners

EMPLOYEES

1972 **3** part-time

1981 150

1981

Major airlines had to bid on
time slots for arrivals and departures
at major airports.

SkyWest was one of five U.S.
airlines to make a profit this year.

Air traffic controllers strike.
President Reagan fired the lot.

Hub and spoke system
of coverage began.

Diversification

A TRADITIONAL PART OF SkyWest HISTORY

From the earliest days, the importance of diversification was not lost on the people of SkyWest. As the core business — passenger airline service — grew, a host of related activities added revenue and maximized the use of resources. These extra efforts included a Piper Aircraft dealership, flight schools and fixed based maintenance operations, as well as flight-seeing tours and charter services. (Charter pilots learned to be especially flexible. Their day's work might consist of anything from transporting illegal aliens to deportation centers in California or shuttling St. George residents to the Mormon Miracle Pageant in Manti, Utah.)

As the company progressed, two primary affiliates emerged—

National Parks Transportation operated a series of rental car agencies; Aviation Services West handled the fixed base operations, charter flights, and sightseeing tours.

By 1992, those enterprises contributed $7.5 million to SkyWest coffers. However, as SkyWest Airlines expanded, a single-minded focus became increasingly important. In 1999, the aviation services were sold. Sale of the rental car agencies occurred the following year. ✈

Acquisition of Palm Springs-based Sun Aire

A SUN AIRE METROLINER OVER PALM SPRINGS AREA

doubled SkyWest's size.

1982 to 1991
THE GROWING YEARS

The ability to adapt, long a SkyWest hallmark, proved vital during a decade when rapid change seemed the aviation industry's only constant. Ever-increasing competition and technological advancements transformed reservation systems, routing techniques, aircraft, even company identities. The era of independent regional carriers serving a small slice of geography was at an end.

SkyWest responded to each innovation with a characteristic balance of can-do optimism and cautious evaluation. Between 1984 and 1986, those qualities enabled it to double in size, become a publicly traded company and add cabin-class flights to a 13-state service area.

A little luck also played a role in the airline's phenomenal growth. Throughout its first decade, SkyWest business lagged in winter. To bolster that season's revenue and maximize equipment, management sought a busy "off-season" warm-weather market. In 1983, it inquired about the possibility of buying Sun Aire, a Palm Springs company flying 19-seat Metroliners to 12 cities in California and Arizona with a corps of non-union pilots. While the size of Sun Aire's coverage area and fleet were similar to SkyWest's, it served a denser population and carried twice as many passengers.

When Sun Aire management said that the owners weren't interested in selling, the SkyWest team decided to start its own Palm Springs operation. In the midst of that station's grand opening, casual conversation indicated that Sun Aire was indeed being sold. SkyWest's management team wondered if it was possible that the deal wasn't final.

SkyWest President Jerry Atkin dialed directory assistance, got the number of the San Francisco-based owner of Sun Aire, and called to see if there was still a chance SkyWest could obtain the airline. Two weeks later, the Atkins — Sid, Ralph and Jerry — met the president of DiGiorgio, the corporation that owned Sun Aire. Six weeks later, with fast financing from Utah's Zion Bank, and personal guarantees from SkyWest board members, the $8 million deal was done.

SkyWest set about combining two vastly different "corporate cultures." It adopted the Palm Spring's airlines' more memorable Official Airline Guide,"OO" code, traded its Republic Airlines Escort reservation system for Sun Aire's more efficient American Airlines Sabre, and developed new marketing strategies and logos. With the merger complete, the SkyWest service area stretched from the Mexican border to Idaho Falls, Idaho, from the beaches of Santa Barbara, California, to the high mesa of Grand Junction, Colorado. The Utah-based company vaulted in size from 42nd to 11th among America's regional carriers. It also possessed the nation's largest fleet of Metroliners and the critical mass necessary to interest Wall Street.

> SkyWest responded to each innovation with a characteristic balance of can-do optimism and cautious evaluation.

Skywest Airlines Celebrates 10 Years

Skywest initiated service in July 1972, serving St. George to Salt Lake City 2 times a day in a small non-pressurized twin engine airplane.

Skywest took delivery of their first Swearingen Metroliner in June 1979. As boardings and number of cities served increased the need for bigger and better equipment became evident.

Now serving 13 cities in 5 states, Sky West operates a fleet of 5 19-passenger Metroliners, 5 Navajo Chieftans and several smaller airplanes used for charter, scenic and special service flights.

It Couldn't Have Been Done Without You

The last decade has witnessed many changes in the entire airline industry, fuel costs rising from pennies a gallon to dollars, mergers of major and commuter/regional carriers alike in an effort to survive, the demise of many carriers, and deregulation. It has truly become a "survival of the fittest" industry. For the past ten years it has been our committment to provide you, our customer, with safe reliable air service.

Our flight schedule is constantly being evaluated and changed in an effort to provide each city we serve with well timed flights for both our interlining and local traveling passengers. Sky West was one of the first commuter/regional carriers in the nation to become a certified air carrier operating under the same rules and regulations as the major carriers. Sometime ago we realized the need for bigger and better airplanes to accomodate our passengers. We now operate five Swearingen Metroliners. The 19 passenger pressurized Metroliner is considered by many to be the most sophisticated airplane used in the commuter/regional airline industry today. Your support has enabled us to grow and expand our system in a planned and orderly fashion. Sky West now serves 13 cities in 5 states with nearly 100 daily flights.

As we look forward to the next 10 years of service our committment of safe reliable service will remain our top priority.

We appreciate your continued support!! Thank you.

Jerry Atkin - Skywest President

SkyWest saluted its community with this ad in the St. George, Utah *Spectrum* on July 4, 1982.

The timing was perfect. New turbo-prop planes designed especially for the rigorous regional air trade were entering the marketplace. They looked and felt like jets, offered smooth rides, enough room to stand up and move around, lavatories and inflight service. To keep competitive SkyWest needed to upgrade its fleet.

Airplanes aren't purchased on a whim. It takes months from order until delivery— longer still to put the craft in service. Each acquisition takes time, energy and lots of money.

To raise capital, SkyWest went public in 1986. The initial offering met resounding suc- cess. When investors snapped up the first 1.25 million shares, another quarter- million were issued. Those sold out too. The resulting $14.5 million in revenue enabled the company to retire outstanding debt, set aside funds for capital improvements and purchase its first turbo-prop—an Embraer Brasilia delivered Christmas Eve of that year. Within a few months, the company ordered 12 more Brasilias and optioned another 16 in a deal worth $150 million.

These heady times seemed all the more exciting when Western Airlines—SkyWest's code sharing partner since 1985—was acquired by Delta. In April 1987, SkyWest became a Delta Connection carrier, partnering with the na- tion's largest airline, offering its passengers easy access to the world.

The same year, *Air Transport World Magazine* selected SkyWest from 500 companies, located throughout the globe, as The Commuter/Re- gional Airline of the Year. SkyWest was cited in part for its ability to "manage mega-growth prof- itably." Upon notification of the award, Jerry Atkin attempted to decline the honor. His ration- ale? The accolades didn't ring true. For the first time in 12 years, SkyWest was losing money. Over- expansion, a highly competitive California market

and a weak national economy had rocked SkyWest's world.

Rapid growth made it impossible for upper management to keep close tabs on all the opera- tions. Employee enthusiasm waned. It was time to get back to basics—to rally everyone around a tra- ditional common goal—to focus on exceptional service to smaller communities.

Toward that end, the cor- porate structure was reorganized and a second management tier established. Employee incentive programs rewarded achievers with stock shares. The highly competitive California side of the business was scrutinized. SkyWest's share of the Golden State market couldn't support the 30-seat Brasilias. It was decided that they'd be better uti- lized serving remote communities in the Intermountain West—Montana and Idaho desti- nations accessed through Delta's Salt Lake City hub. Because these markets already benefited from Delta's infrastructure, the tactic required little investment. The more economical Metroliners became SkyWest's hard working California commuters. While its competitors ordered more planes, SkyWest held pat.

The strategy worked. By the first quarter of 1988, SkyWest was back in the black. In 1990, at a time when the Iraqi invasion of Kuwait sent fuel prices soaring and airlines staggering at the added expense, SkyWest posted record revenues. That year it netted a healthy profit and awarded nearly half a million dollars in employee bonuses.

SkyWest stayed the course, striving to meet ever-increasing levels of quality while keeping an eye on the future. As its second decade drew to a close, SkyWest's first ever five-year plan called for phasing out the 19-seat Metroliners in favor of an "all-cabin class" fleet of Brasilias and small jets. Common sense would dictate if and when that vision could be realized. ✦

SkyWest Airlines' Fairchild 19-passenger "Metro," bearing variation of Western Airlines colors and logo, is one of 33 carrier uses to serve 34 destinations in eight western states.

Directors and officers of Skywest Airlines, above left to right, include John Listermoet, J. Ralph Atkin, Janice Hardy, Earl B. Snow, John C. Bowler, Ron B. Reber, Mike Callahan, Sidney J. Atkin and Jerry C. Atkin, president. Jerry C. Atkin, left, sees record revenues and earnings ahead for the carrier in the present fiscal year. Skywest is adding six, $5-million, 30-passenger "Brasilia," below, to its fleet. Ten years ago it had only four, nine-passenger aircraft and was nearly bankrupt.

Tribune Photos by Robert H. Woody
Page Design by Rhonda Hailes

Up and Down the Street

SkyWest Owners Flying High After Stock Sale

ST. GEORGE — With 65 percent of the shares still in their control after a public offering earlier this year, the Atkin family of St. George and four close associates are very much in the pilot's seat of SkyWest Inc.

And with some $3.4 million of debt eliminated and $2.3 million in new equipment purchases begun with the $11,269,000 in proceeds, the firm's subsidiary SkyWest Airlines Inc. is flying higher and farther and faster as a commuter and feeder carrier for 34 destinations in eight western states.

Robert H. Woody
Business Editor

And it is far recovered from the financial nose dive that nearly took it into bankruptcy a decade ago.

While its first-quarter earnings were down from the year-ago quarter when it enjoyed record revenues — inflated in part by the United Airlines strike and by two competitors dropping out — it still expects full-year earnings to top the record $2,446,000 it earned for the 1986 year ending March 31, says SkyWest President Jerry C. Atkin.

That expectation includes record per-share earnings as well — even after the dilution occasioned by the public offering, which resulted in SkyWest Inc. being listed on the national-over-the-counter market (NASDAQ)

Among reasons:

— Delivery of the first three of six Brazilian-made 30-passenger "Brasilia" aircraft SkyWest has ordered.

— The prospective merger of Delta Airlines, and Western Airlines with whom SkyWest has a joint marketing agreement.

The $5 million Brasilia, while prop-driven, has the amenities of a jet, including overhead storage, a lavatory and passenger flight attendant as part of the crew.

These pressurized aircraft will increase capacity, convenience and range of SkyWest.

Since April, SkyWest has had the joint mar-

keting arrangement with Western, which, in effect — at least from passenger perception — has made SkyWest an extension of the Los Angeles-based Western when it comes to booking flights.

SkyWest now flies under the colors and logo of "Western Express." While the loss of identity is, indeed, a bit troublesome for an independent that wants to enlarge its stock market presence, the enhancement of revenues and profits by the Western association more than overcomes any disadvantage, Mr. Atkin says.

And those revenues and profits should be even further enhanced by the merger of Western and Delta, he says.

The boards of Western and Delta have given their approval. But additional approvals are required of stockholders and the Department of Transportation.

And because the Atlanta-based Delta has international flights to Europe, the president of the United States must also give his approval.

An optimistic scenario could see the merger completed sometime between December and spring.

Depending upon whether Texas Air is able to pull off its acquisition of People Express, Frontier and Eastern Airlines, the surviving Delta would end up as either third- or fourth-largest carrier in the nation.

In either case it would be largest carrier in the Western United States — a major benefit to SkyWest which 10 years ago was sputtering toward a Chapter 11. It barely pulled out by working out extensions with its creditors. And in 1976, it turned a $17,000 profit — its first ever — on revenues of $1 million.

At that time SkyWest had a fleet of four nine-passenger $280,000 twin-engine Navajo Chieftains providing service between St. George; Cedar City; Salt Lake City; Page, Ariz.; and Las Vegas

It now owns or leases 35 Metro II and Metro III Fairchild aircraft with 17- and 19-passenger capacity. Its fleet also includes 17 Cessna 207s, a twin-engine Navajo and a helicopter at Page, Ariz., where it provides most of the Grand Canyon river-running delivery and pick-up flight services.

The firm also has subsidiary car-rental businesses in Cedar City, Vernal, Page and Ely, Nev.

See F-2, Column 5

This newspaper article appeared in *The Salt Lake Tribune* on October 26, 1986.

I'd Rather be Flying
SkyWest Airlines

All passengers aboard SkyWest flights on June 19, 1982 received pins and bumper stickers to commemorate the company's 10th anniversary.

THE CHAIRMAN
OF THE
CIVIL AERONAUTICS BOARD
WASHINGTON, D. C. 20428

May 17, 1982

Dear Jerry:

Thanks for the fine tour of your facilities.

Frankly, I was genuinely impressed with your operation, your people, your training, marketing and the overall way you've jumped into the Ely and Elko essential air service program.

Just keep up the good work.

Best regards,

Dan McKinnon

SkyWest's dedicated employees grew with the company. Donna Jardine Law joined the company as a ticket agent, rose through the ranks, and eventually became Director of Marketing.

Mr. Jerry C. Atkin
President
Skywest Airlines
St. George Municipal Airport
P.O. Box T
St. George, Utah 84770

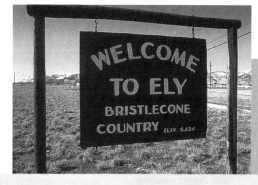

The Nevada communities of Elko and Ely were less than enthusiastic when SkyWest entered the market after United Airlines pulled out. However, in 1982, after Civil Aeronautics Board Chairman Dan McKinnon visited the fledgling SkyWest operations there, the Elko/Ely route was permanently awarded to SkyWest.

1982

SkyWest joined Republic Airlines Escort computer reservation system.

Each month 3,000 SkyWest passengers connected to Western Airlines flights in Salt Lake City.

June 19: 10th Anniversary of initial flight

Western Airlines chose Salt Lake City as its hub.

> ❝With deregulation there was an explosion of opportunity.❞
>
> — RON REBER, CHIEF OPERATING OFFICER

PREMIERING OCTOBER 15!
Direct From Carson City!

SkyWest Airlines

Now Skywest metroliner is the fastest, most economical and most convenient way to travel between Carson City and Las Vegas.

SCHEDULE

TO CARSON CITY		FROM CARSON CITY	
Depart 9:00 a.m.	Arrive 10:30 a.m.	Depart 7:15 a.m.	Arrive 8:45 a.m.
Depart 6:00 p.m.	Arrive 7:30 p.m.	Depart 4:10 p.m.	Arrive 5:40 p.m.

FOR INFORMATION AND RESERVATIONS CALL YOUR TRAVEL AGENT OR SKY WEST

TOLL FREE   1-800-453-9417

FAST FACTS: SkyWest was hard pressed to establish a customer service presence when it entered the Carson City, Nevada, market in 1984. The air terminal had been converted into a tavern, and the proprietor wasn't interested in giving up his lease. So SkyWest rented a portion of the bar, and the agent wrote tickets on the counter.

SkyWest as Western Express served Jackson, Wyoming, c. 1985.

CODE SHARING, COMPUTERIZED RESERVATION SYSTEMS, AND THE DEMISE OF THE INDEPENDENT REGIONAL AIRLINE

A regional airline's dependency upon a major carrier began with computer reservation systems, and intensified with the implementation of code sharing agreements. Computerized reservations meant the major airline controlling the system could make it easier for travel agents to book an entire trip on one airline—their own. The regional airline, considered an "interline" carrier, was at a disadvantage. As the major carriers ceased doing business in smaller communities, "regionals" hustled to shuttle passengers to hub airports served by the larger companies. Major airlines recognizing the importance of these "feeder" planes, allowed specific regional partners to share their airline "code"—the means by which the airline was identified in the travel agency "bible"—the Official Airline Guide. Code sharing evened the reservations playing field, but further eroded the regional airline's identity.

In 1982, SkyWest signed on with Republic Airline's Escort computer reservation system. With the Sun Aire acquisition the more efficient American Airlines Sabre system was put in place. The company resisted code sharing until it considered all its options, and finally signed on as a Western Express carrier in Salt Lake City in 1985. When that airline was acquired by Delta, a year later, SkyWest found itself partnered with what was at that time the nation's largest air carrier.

1983   SkyWest was ranked 42nd among the top 100 U.S. regional carriers.

Hub and spoke routing relationships made regional carriers more dependent upon a "code-share" with major airline partners.

September, 1982

October, 1982

March, 1983

June, 1983

October, 1984

February, 1985

April, 1985

July, 1985

who *appreciate* them." – RON REBER, CHIEF OPERATING OFFICER

November, 1985

April, 1986

March, 1987

As these timetables indicate, during its second decade, SkyWest evolved dramatically from a small Utah operation to a code-sharing ally of Western Airlines to the regional partner of Delta, an airline that spanned the globe.

1987

1994

❝ We never thought code sharing would come to the West. We were negotiating a merger with WingsWest in '85 and then, overnight they cut a deal with American Airlines to become that airline's regional partner. After exploring all the options we went with Western. ❞

– RON REBER,
CHIEF OPERATING OFFICER

Utah's Zion's Bank took less than 30 days to arrange the $8 million financing needed for the Sun Aire acquisition. All the SkyWest board members personally guaranteed the loan.

Board members gather to celebrate the Sun Aire acquisition. (Standing l to r) Harold Chesler, Steve Udvar-Hazy, Dell Stout, Sid Atkin, Lee Atkin, Merv Cox, (sitting l to r) Jerry Atkin, Ralph Atkin, Brett Atkin.

After the 1984 Sun Aire acquisition, SkyWest set about merging two corporate cultures and personas. When the airline became a Western Express carrier in 1985, it added another identity as evidenced by the multiple logos adorning the plane shown above.

1984

SkyWest acquired Palm Springs-based Sun Aire.

The Sun Aire-SkyWest combined fleet of 31 Metroliners was the world's largest.

Val Williams became vice president of maintenance.

SkyWest became the 11th largest regional airline in the U.S.

Last Navajo airplane was retired.

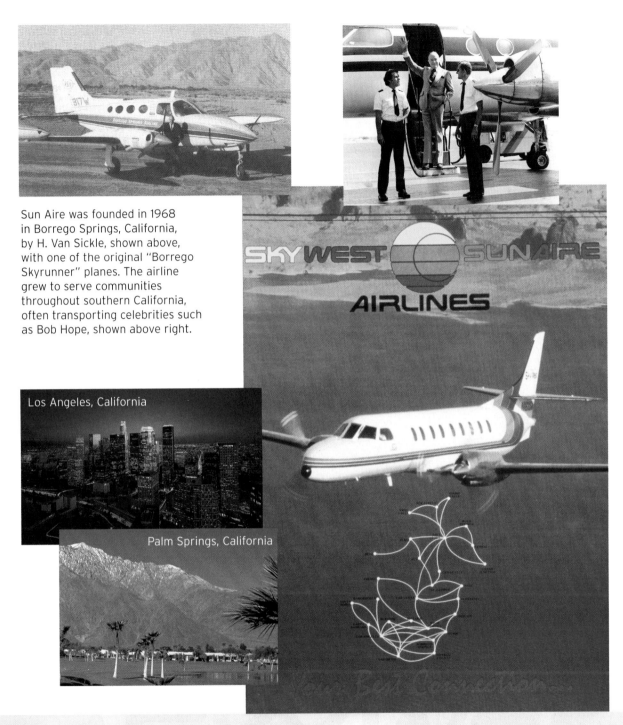

Sun Aire was founded in 1968 in Borrego Springs, California, by H. Van Sickle, shown above, with one of the original "Borrego Skyrunner" planes. The airline grew to serve communities throughout southern California, often transporting celebrities such as Bob Hope, shown above right.

Los Angeles, California

Palm Springs, California

A code sharing agreement with Western Airlines made SkyWest a Western Express carrier.

1985

SkyWest executive offices moved from the maintenance hangar to downtown St. George.

October: Western Airlines started listing SkyWest's Salt Lake City flights as its own in the Official Airline Guide.

The Turbo-prop Embraer Brasilia,

enhanced reliability and efficiency.

INITIAL PUBLIC OFFERING MAKES TURBO-PROP PURCHASE POSSIBLE

Turbo-props spawned another regional aviation revolution. The pressurized "cabin-class" planes featured plenty of "stand-up" headroom, and lavatories. They also combined the exceptional reliability of the jet engine with the operating efficiency of a propeller-powered plane. Cruising altitudes of 20,000 feet made for smooth flying. After evaluating several planes, SkyWest's settled on a product made by Embraer of Brazil, aptly named the Brasilia. The company used proceeds from the initial public offering for its purchase.

When Earl Snow and Klen Brooks brought the first turbo-prop home from Brazil on Christmas Eve, 1986, they'd covered 5,500 nautical miles in 48-hours—start to finish. A crowd made up of townspeople from every walk of life welcomed them at the St. George airport. Many of the well-wishers had also been on hand for SkyWest's inaugural open house, as well as the arrival of the first Navajo and the Metroliner.

> "Before the Sun Aire acquisition, we flew air-planes nobody liked to places no one wanted to go. With Sun Aire all that changed and we became a short-haul feeder. It changed the way we viewed the entire airline business."
>
> – JAN NELSON,
> FORMER CORPORATE SECRETARY,
> IN *TIME FLIES, THE HISTORY OF SKYWEST AIRLINES.*

1986

Initial Public Stock offering raised $14.5 million.

Palm Springs facility underwent $3.5 million expansion.

December 24: the first 30-seat Brasilia arrived in St. George, Utah.

Code sharing resulted in a traffic increase of almost 50%.

The Salt Lake City Tribune reported SkyWest's good fortune on April 19, 1987.

The Salt Lake Tribune

Busi

Chairman J. Ralph Atkin, front, and Gary Goodman, St. George maintenan

Up and Down the Street

SkyWest Airlines Soars On the Wings of Delta-Western Merger

ST. GEORGE — A year and a half ago, SkyWest Airlines, St. George-based commuter carrier, could not have dreamed it ... be an affiliate of one of the largest ... United States.

gar at St. George its first Metroliner bearing its new white, blue and red stripes..

It followed by only a few days Delta's full embrace of Western, for more than 50 years an independent carrier with commercial and cultural links to Salt Lake City.

... based Western

GIVING TALENT A CHANCE PAYS OFF

In the early '80s, Pocatello, Idaho, station manager Ron Reber worked hard to drum up travel agent business. At one agency, the SkyWest representative was especially impressed by the knowledge and enthusiasm of the owner's teenage son, Steve Hart. "He had this incredible fascination with schedules and routing. He'd even created a virtual airline with a hub and spoke system, before it was an industry standard."

Within seven years, Reber was Vice President of SkyWest marketing and Steve Hart was a SkyWest sales representative calling on travel agents. He hadn't lost his passion for perfectly coordinated arrivals and departures, however. "We were losing money with the Brasilias," Reber said. "Steve was pretty sure he could come up with a way of meshing our schedules with Delta's arrivals and departures to make those Brasilias work for us." So, Reber convinced upper management to give Hart a chance at revising the entire system — even though he wasn't even part of the scheduling department.

Steve Hart

Ron Reber

Creating the plan took three months. "It was before we used computers for that sort of thing. He had charts all over the walls," Reber recalls. Hart also had an infectious enthusiasm and tactics that ultimately worked. The Brasilias were moved to Montana and Idaho where their arrivals and departures were coordinated with those of Delta Airlines. SkyWest's revenues started to climb. "Strategically, it was masterful," Reber said.

1987

- Seventeen flight attendants joined SkyWest's ranks.
- Delta Airlines acquired Western Airlines, making it the nation's largest carrier.
- February 1: Brasilia service began in Palm Springs.
- April 1: SkyWest became a Delta Connection partner.
- October: Stock market crashed

Jerry Atkin accepts the Regional Airline of the Year Award from the previous recipient, George Pickett, president of Atlantic Southeast Airlines, another Delta Connection partner.

I've got CONNECTIONS! SKYWEST AIRLINES

1987 Commuter/Regional Airline of the Year SkyWest Airlines Presented by Air Transport World Annual Airline Awards Program

In 1987, SkyWest's San Francisco hub shuttled passengers to California cities – Monterey, San Luis Obispo, Santa Maria, Sacramento, Paso Robles, and Fresno. By then, the SkyWest system stretched from the Mexican border to Idaho Falls, Idaho, and from the Pacific Ocean to Grand Junction, Colorado.

Third quarter losses ended SkyWest's 12-year profitability streak.

1987

Air Transport World selected SkyWest Commuter/Regional Airline of the Year from 500 regional airlines worldwide.

Longest route segment – Palm Springs to Salt Lake City – was 500 miles nonstop.

For the first time in 12 years, SkyWest lost money in 1987. The downturn was short-lived. The company combatted the negative effects of over-expansion, a highly competitive California market and a floundering national economy with a back-to-basics business strategy. As part of the plan, corporate structure was re-organized, and an additional level of management put in place. In 1988, Sid and Ralph Atkin stepped down from active management but retained their positions on the board. That body included (l to r) Keith Malnar, John Bowler, Earl Snow, Sid Atkin, Ralph Atkin, Jerry Atkin, Jan Nelson, Eric Christensen, Mike Callahan.

> " When I look at the management people, I take **great pride** in their development. They were all local St. George people and now they are **leaders in the industry.** If I played any part in that, it's a proud achievement. "

– RALPH ATKIN, FOUNDER

1988

SkyWest posted a profit.

Ralph Atkin and Sid Atkin retired as officers of the company.

Airline doubled in size.

March: Short Bros. Aircraft, a legend in aviation, and associate of the Wright Brothers, developed a small regional jet and was soon acquired by Canada's Bombardier.

From the **Pacific** to the **Rockies** SkyWest

The Pacific Coast, California

Country expanded to cover the West.

The Sawtooth Mountains, Idaho

In 1991, after evaluating the possibility of moving headquarters to a larger market, it was decided that SkyWest would continue to make its home in St. George, Utah. The same year, company leaders unveiled a model of the $3.6 million, 63,000 square-foot corporate office building planned for 15-acres in St. George. Pictured below with model, from left, Brad Rich, Eric Christensen, Rob Reber, Mike Callahan, Jerry Atkin, and Mike Kraupp

Eric Christensen was hired to help prepare the company for its first public stock offering in 1986. He became Vice-President of Planning five years later. At the same time, Ron Reber became Vice-President of Customer Service and Marketing, John Ligtermoet was named Senior Vice-President of Operations, Brad Rich became Senior Vice-President of Finance and Chief Financial Officer, John Bowler became Treasurer, and Mike Callahan became Vice-President of Human Resources.

St. George, Utah

1989

One million passengers flown

Five year plan included jets complementing turbo-props.

1990

August invasion of Iraq resulted in fuel price hike from $.77 to $1.40 per gallon

SkyWest becomes first U.S. airline to option a Canadair Regional Jet.

May: First annual meeting for employees and families.

San Diego, California

SkyWest orders placed during 1988 and 1989 for 11 Metroliner IIIs kept the manufacturer's production line busy for an entire year.

In 1991, SkyWest Metroliners shuttled between LAX in Los Angeles and San Diego every 35 minutes.

This new $4 million maintenance hangar at Salt Lake City International Airport opened in 1991.

> " SkyWest is successful because our people are resourceful and **not afraid of failure.** If you make a mistake and learn from it, that's OK. We'll just fix it. That's always been the attitude. "
>
> – RON REBER, CHIEF OPERATING OFFICER

1991

High fuel costs contributed to the bankruptcy of four major airlines, including Continental and Pan Am.

High fuel prices added $500,000 per month in costs – potentially wiping out annual profits.

Delta service spanned the globe.

New $4 million maintenance hangar opened in Salt Lake City.

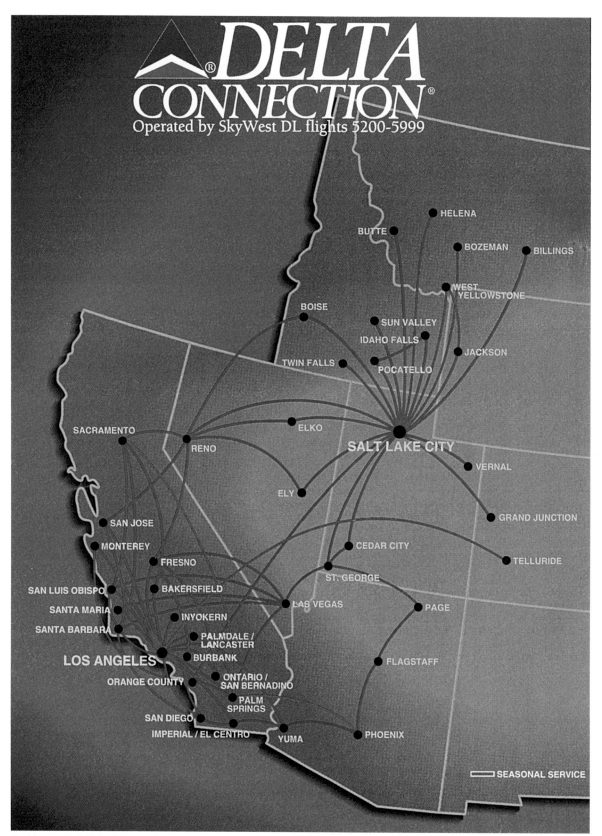

By the end of 1991, SkyWest as Delta Connection blanketed the West.

DESTINATIONS

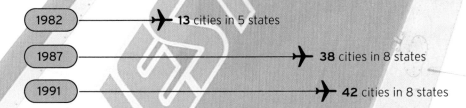

1982 ✈ **13** cities in 5 states

1987 ✈ **38** cities in 8 states

1991 ✈ **42** cities in 8 states

PLANES

1982 ✈ **8** – 4 Metroliners, 4 Navajos

1987 ✈ **31** – World's largest fleet of Metroliners

1991 ✈ **46** – 15 Embraer Brasilias, 35 Metroliners

EMPLOYEES

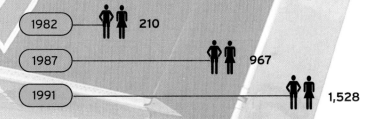

1982 **210**

1987 **967**

1991 **1,528**

PASSENGERS

1982 **81,000**

1987 **796,173**

1991 **1,094,368**

Safety

ALWAYS A PRIORITY AT SKYWEST AIRLINES

SkyWest made safety a top priority from day one. The maintenance department's attention to detail and eye for prevention paid off. For almost fifteen years, the airline operated without a serious incident. During that time only three minor occurrences marred a perfect record — none involved injuries.

That all changed on January 15, 1987 over Kearns, Utah, when a student pilot accompanied by an instructor collided at 2,800 feet above ground with a SkyWest Metroliner arriving from Pocatello, Idaho. Among the ten fatalities — SkyWest Captain

Michael E. Gambill, and First Officer Walter F. Ray. Later, officials would find the flight instructor and control tower at blame. Exoneration offered little comfort to the people of SkyWest.

Six weeks after a Utah court faulted the controller for the 1987 Kearns' collision, SkyWest was again a victim of circumstances. On February 1, 1991, SkyWest — an airline with an incredible safety record, operating one of the newest fleets in the industry — suffered tragedy through no fault of its own.

SkyWest flight 5569 had been sched-

DESERET NEWS, FRIDAY, JANUARY 16, 1987 **A 3**

Crash doesn't shake official's confidence in SkyWest Airlines

By Max B. Knudson
Deseret News business editor

The loss Thursday of a SkyWest Airlines Fairchild Metroliner in a collision with a private plane over Kearns was a tragedy, but the chairman of the Utah Air Travel Commission told the Deseret News the accident has not shaken his faith in the St. George-based regional carrier.

ly departures, including 43 at Salt Lake City International Airport and 101 at Los Angeles International Airport — more than any other carrier at LAX.

The airline carried 762,773 passengers during 1986, as well as 100 tons of cargo.

While the commission has been primarily concerned with the quality and frequency of Utah air service, said air safety "has always been a uled to depart Los Angeles at 5:45 bound for Palmdale, 50 miles away. The control tower advised Captain Andy Lucas to wait on runway 24Left until a WingsWest flight crossed that runway on its way to the terminal. The skies were clear, but the sun had set as a USAir 737-300 carrying 89 people — passengers and crew — was cleared to land at runway 24Right. However, as that craft approached Los Angeles, the control tower requested that it switch and make a visual landing on runway 24Left — where SkyWest flight 5569 still waited takeoff clearance.

The USAir pilot did not see the Metroliner until his plane was almost on the runway. The collision occurred at 6:04 p.m. All 10 passengers and two crew members aboard the SkyWest plane were lost. They included Captain Lucas, First Officer Frank Prentice III, as well as Palmdale Station Manager Mike Fuller and Randy Wilburn, husband of Palmdale customer service representative Carolyn Wilburn. Among the casualties aboard the 737 were its captain, Colin Shaw and flight attendant Deanna Bethea.

As the entire SkyWest "family" grieved, Jerry Atkin offered encouragement. "We've been dealt a tough one here," he said. "This simply tests our mettle but this challenge is not going to be bigger than we are. It just makes us stronger."

The National Transportation Safety Board (NTSB) placed full responsibility for the incident on the Federal Aviation Administration. Neither SkyWest nor the local controller was cited. The FAA had failed to provide adequate policy direction and oversight, according to the NTSB. ⬡

Freight

AN IMPORTANT SERVICE

Cargo has long been an important part of SkyWest service. America's rail and bus services were deregulated around the same time as the nation's airlines. So, the smaller communities looked to regional carriers to handle freight. SkyWest got the job done. In 1982, at a time when it ranked 17th among commuters in terms of passenger boarding it was the number three freight carrier — hauling 1,236,346 pounds!

In 2000, the airline implemented SkyShip service to track packages shipped via SkyWest Cargo. ⬡

A commitment to quality, honesty

and **integrity** paid off.

THE EMBRAER BRASILIA, PAINTED TO COMMEMORATE
SKYWEST AIRLINES' 25TH ANNIVERSARY, IN 1997.

1992 to 2001
THE QUALITY YEARS

In 1993, SkyWest embarked on its third decade, a well-respected public company doing big business from expansive new headquarters. The pride of St. George, Utah didn't rest on its laurels, however. Instead it looked to the future, devising a strategy to retire all Metroliners and convert the fleet to cabin-class planes within four years. As the aviation industry struggled with circumstances beyond its control, realizing that goal would take some doing.

In the aftermath of the 1992 Gulf War, fuel prices remained high and the economy stayed weak. Too many airlines sought a piece of the California commuter market. Southwest Airlines, the revolutionary low-frills, discount carrier, complicated matters. While it didn't attempt to serve SkyWest's outlying destinations, Southwest's low prices enticed passengers to drive to major hubs, bypassing regional service.

To meet the California challenge, SkyWest restructured management, reorganized its fleet and intensified efforts to reach business travelers with common sense pricing innovations.

The tactics met with some success. When Southwest's bargain-basement pricing entered a market, most other airlines lost 7% to 8% of their business. SkyWest losses hovered around 1%.

Major airlines also theorized that the economical 50-seat Regional Jets could help them maintain a presence in markets where discount carriers cut into business. However, when SkyWest took possession of its first two Canadair Regional Jets in 1994, it was with the notion of avoiding areas targeted by low-fare competition. The plane's speed — 530 miles per hour — ideally served cities located approximately 400 miles from Salt Lake City where the company flourished. SkyWest's regional jet service effectively enhanced the healthy side of its business and helped offset the weaker markets.

Creativity helped SkyWest improve the situation in California — an environment where major airlines such as SkyWest's code sharing partner Delta — suffered even more than regionals did. First, SkyWest persuaded Delta to allow Continental to become an additional code-sharing partner on some Delta Connection flights. This filled some of SkyWest's excess capacity with Continental passengers. However, it wasn't enough to gain SkyWest a greater share of a crowded market during a stressful time for all of aviation.

Airlines over-booked to meet a soaring increase in travel. There weren't enough runways to comfortably accommodate demand. Air traffic controllers habitually favored major carriers in landings and takeoff sequences. A series of unrelated incidents involving regional carriers tarnished the entire industry's safety reputation. Turbo-props came under intense scrutiny. The FAA explored restricting the use of certain models in extreme weather conditions. Amid the hubbub, the public decided they'd rather drive than fly on a "puddle jumper." The Metros, long the workhorse of SkyWest Airlines, had to go.

January 1, 1997, SkyWest converted to an all-cabin-class fleet. Shortly thereafter, acting out of necessity, SkyWest decided to take a shot at developing a relationship with United Airlines. Ron Reber had a contact, Paula Barbieri, in the United tariff department. He made a call. Unbeknownst to the SkyWest team, the timing was perfect. United was unhappy with the performance of its west coast code-sharing partner. Barbieri knew SkyWest's solid reputation. Wheels were set in motion. Negotiations began. SkyWest was attempting the impossible — code sharing with two competing major airlines.

Rick Egan/The Salt Lake Tribune

SkyWest President Jerry Atkin says regional fleet's backbone remains turboprop planes, but jets may be on horizon.

SkyWest, Bustling at 20, Reaches Growth Crossroads

Airline's Corporate Pilot Hedges Bets, Trims Fat

By John Keahey
THE SALT LAKE TRIBUNE

ST. GEORGE — SkyWest Airlines President Jerry Atkin says he has to check his ego.

The head of this highly successful regional airline, tucked away in sparsely populated southwest Utah, has watched misplaced egos drive carrier after carrier out of business.

The vision of sleek passenger jets flying out of tiny airports grew bigger than ticket sales.

Twenty-year-old SkyWest is at that crossroads. It should either move into larger markets — and larger, more expensive aircraft — or continue to do what it does so well: shuttle passengers from tiny Intermountain West and Southern California communities to and from Salt Lake City and Los Angeles.

"If we ignore our core business and jump completely into jets, it could break us," Mr. Atkins fears.

SkyWest is one of the more successful airlines in an industry decimated by nearly three years of steep losses. It and other regional airlines are making money while the major carriers — Delta, TWA, American — pile up multimillion-dollar losses.

Last quarter, the regional airline earned $1.6 million on $35 million in revenues. Mr. Atkins expects it to do at least that well when second-quarter results are released in a few weeks.

"We may come to the conclusion we can make money flying to Pocatello and to hell with jets," Mr. Atkin says bluntly.

He and his staff know that now is not the time to make such a decision. The domestic airlines industry is in disarray, licking its wounds in the aftermath of vicious fare wars and is trying to deal with a cranky U.S. economy. Most observers predict things will calm down by middecade.

To hedge its bet, SkyWest has taken ouf nonbinding op-

■ See D-6, Column 4

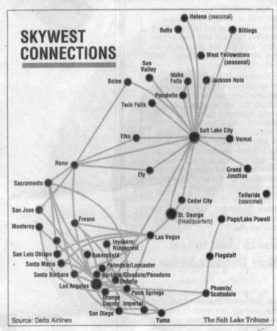

SKYWEST CONNECTIONS

Source: Delta Airlines   The Salt Lake Tribune

In 1992, at a time when the national airline industry was in "disarray," the *Salt Lake City Tribune* recognized SkyWest's 20th anniversary with this article underscoring the company's long-standing philosophy of fiscal caution.

United proposed to enter into a "fee-for-departure" contract. SkyWest would essentially lease its aircraft and crew to United. The major airline would assume all the risk, as well as responsibility for pricing, ticketing and seat inventories.

The only hurdle? SkyWest's commitment to Delta. As always, honesty and straightforwardness paid off. The St. George-based airline needed to retain its strong Salt Lake City base, while increasing its California business. To appease its original code-sharing partner, SkyWest kept operating as Delta Connection in eight southern California cities while dedicating other planes to United Express passengers.

By October of 1997, SkyWest was operating 68 daily Los Angeles flights as a Delta Connection and 120 as United Express. It opened 12 new cities in 90 days, ordered more Brasilias and regional jets to accommodate ever-increasing demand, and learned what it's like to run two distinct airline operations.

The transition was not without obstacles. United's pilot contract limited the number of jets a code-sharing partner could fly and severely restricted the regional jets entry into California. SkyWest expanded its fleet of California-based Brasilias. Each new plane required at least 35 new employees. Hiring, training, and ordering aircraft became a regular part of day-to-day operations. Route maps seemingly changed with each turn of the calendar. Delta Connection service pushed across the border to Vancouver, British Columbia. United Express planes shuttled approximately 3 million passengers annually.

By 2000, Delta Connection operated by SkyWest flew as far east as Minneapolis. That year, another stock offering raised $122.4 million, and industry analysts touted SkyWest as the fastest growing regional airline "in the universe".

The fee-for-departure system became the topic of SkyWest's talks with Delta. However, shortly after negotiations were agreed upon, the world turned upside down.

On September 11, 2001, terrorists hijacked four east coast jetliners. Two were used as missiles crashing into New York's World Trade Center towers. A third was flown into the Pentagon. The fourth slammed into a Pennsylvania field after passengers foiled hijacker plans. Before the debris cleared, the death toll exceeded 2,500. While less significant, the loss of property seemed incalculable.

As the tragedy unfolded, the FAA halted all traffic in U.S. air space. One hundred and seventeen airborne SkyWest planes immediately headed for the nearest airport. By the time the second WTC tower collapsed, every SkyWest plane and passenger was safely on the ground. The air travel moratorium lasted four days. On Friday, September 15, 75% of SkyWest's planes were in operation. By Monday almost the entire fleet was flying again.

The anguish associated with that date cannot be measured in degrees. However, the use of commercial aircraft to perpetrate such unimaginable horror meant severe and long-lasting consequences for aviation. In the weeks following the tragedy, air-travel declined by more than 50%. The industry reacted to huge losses by laying off more than 100,000 employees — a fifth of all workers. Security concerns further complicated the business.

SkyWest's financial conservatism served the company well. With ample cash reserves SkyWest weathered the storm. Despite canceling nearly 3,800 flights in the weeks following the tragedy, and retiring eight Brasilias earlier than planned, the airline avoided company-wide furloughs.

Day by day, the major airlines re-invented themselves. United pulled out of six markets completely and was replaced by partners such as SkyWest. Delta retained its market presence but reduced flight frequency, allowing regional carriers to step in with smaller planes. Both tactics meant increased opportunity for SkyWest. Despite a disastrous second half, SkyWest's 2001 earnings dropped only 7% to $56 million, while revenues increased 15% to $602 million.

SkyWest's prosperity contributed to strained relationships with its struggling major partners. To mitigate the situation, SkyWest worked hard to lower costs while continuing to elevate quality. ✈

The Salt Lake Tribune

BUSINESS

SECTION
E
SUNDAY

JET CURRIER, E-3 ■ HUMBERTO CRUZ, E-4

JULY 9, 2000

Steve Griffin/The Salt Lake Tribune

A SkyWest Airlines' pilot gives his turboprop aircraft an inspection at the Salt Lake International Airport prior to a morning flight to St. George on June 28.

Shuttle Diplomacy

SkyWest Airlines carved its niche in the sky by linking routes for Delta, United

BY PHIL SAHM

THE SALT LAKE TRIBUNE

ST. GEORGE — Jerry Atkin may not have known it then, but fortune was on his side in 1975.

Atkin, in his mid-20s, had just joined SkyWest Airlines, a commuter line his uncle started in 1972 with the idea of connecting St. George to other cities in the West. But after three tough years, the airline had amounted to little more than a wing and a prayer — with an increasing emphasis on prayer.

In debt, with its expenses mounting, the airline looked certain to fail. So Atkin and his uncle, St. George attorney Ralph Atkin, hoped to convince another small carrier, Sun Valley Key Airlines, to buy SkyWest for $25,000.

No sale.

The Sun Valley airline also was just eking by. Desperate, the Atkins offered to let go of SkyWest for nothing.

"We couldn't give it away," recalls Jerry Atkin, now chairman and chief executive officer of SkyWest's parent company, SkyWest Inc.

Declaring bankruptcy was not an option — family pride would not allow it — and that left no choice but to make the company succeed.

In retrospect, Atkin must feel fortunate that the one airline he and his uncle approached could not afford to take SkyWest — even for free. It did not come easy, but SkyWest slowly turned around and 25 years later has become the fourth-largest regional airline in the country.

More than luck has guided this company. Industry experts say SkyWest is one of the best-run airlines in the industry.

With one of the longest-serving management teams of any airline, SkyWest has landed in a spot few regional carriers reach: It serves as a feeder airline to hubs of two of the largest carriers in the country — United Airlines and Delta Air Lines. Those contracts have propelled SkyWest's growth and, in the case of United, given the regional airline what any business prizes: guaranteed revenue.

And the company is poised for more growth.

See **SKYWEST**, Page E-5

Small Airline Grows Up

SkyWest Airlines has leveraged its relationships with Delta Air Lines and United Airlines to become the fourth-largest regional carrier in the country. While the company has staked its claim in the West, new routes into Denver have opened the potential for expansion into the Midwest and farther east.

Source: SkyWest Airlines

Sean Noyce/The Salt Lake Tribune

By 2000, when this *Salt Lake City Tribune* article heralded its accomplishments, SkyWest had successfully operated as Delta Connection and United Express for three years.

Management

DESTINATION EXCELLENCE

Delta Connection SkyWest has recaptured its Number One ranking in Southern California and is banking on superior service to keep it there.

By ARNOLD LEWIS

SkyWest Airlines in March received more complimentary letters than complaints from its passengers for the first time in its 20-year history—63 to 59, to be exact.

That is an extraordinary achievement in an industry plagued with flight cancellations and delays, lost baggage, and often overworked and quick-tempered passenger-service agents. It's also a key to the story of how a large regional airline went about growing from adolescence into maturity.

Simply stated, SkyWest has altered its corporate culture. It has transformed itself from an operation ented company to one that focus service. Such dramatic c required a reorganization at th top and all the pain that goes with it. It also required the de ment of an employee motivation gram unique in the regional

Major Brasilia maintenance is underway in the new $5 million maintenance and training facility at Salt Lake City. The facility is staffed by 45 mechanics and includes individual engine and accessory shops. Most avionics maintenance is performed at the carrier's Palm Springs, California maintenance base. The primary hangar can handle eight Brasilias or 13 Metro IIIs at one time or a combination of the two. The second-floor contains classrooms for varied uses.

The Destination Excellence Program encouraged all employees to "do the right thing" in an effort to exceed customer expectations. Supervisors and frequent flyers presented "High Five" certificates, worth $5 at the company store, to employees caught in the act of excellence. It was part of a successful strategy aimed at keeping SkyWest a company driven by the needs of its customers. The effort was featured in this *Business and Commercial Aviation* magazine.

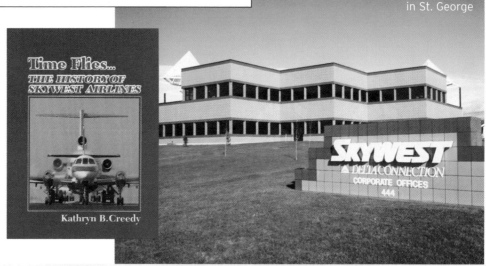

$3.6 miillion corporate offices in St. George

In conjunction with the company's 20th anniversary, a history of the airline by noted aviation author, Kathryn Creedy, was published.

Time Flies... THE HISTORY OF SKYWEST AIRLINES
Kathryn B. Creedy

1992

Construction began on new $3.6 million corporate offices.

1993

Destination Excellence Program implemented to inspire employees to higher level of service and quality

Creative pricing plan offered a variety of fares and maximized capacity.

> **"** We've never had a vision to grow for growth's sake. Company's that do that can get in trouble. Sometimes you have a bad year, and you just have to batten down and do nothing. If you have a quality vision — do a good job for customers and share-holders — then I believe you get the chance to grow. From our quality came the quantity. **"**
>
> — JERRY ATKIN

VARIETY OF FARES MAXIMIZED CAPACITY

Common-sense principles helped SkyWest abandon archaic "yield management" pricing strategies in 1993 — three years ahead of the rest of the industry. This long-standing practice severely restricted the number of discount seats on each flight, because airlines tried to maximize the dollar "yield" of each seat, without considering the over-all revenue generated by an entire planeload of people. Therefore, planes sometimes flew with empty high-priced seats. SkyWest's inno-vative strategy made those seats available at lower prices in order to fill the flight.

SkyWest passengers were afforded easy access to the world, when Delta, the nation's largest airline, became an international force after the bankruptcy of Pan American Airlines.

Plan implemented to convert fleet to all cabin class within four years.

Total market value of company stock exceeded $100 million for first time.

Business passengers comprised 65% of total traffic.

The Canadair Regional Jet offered

Delta Connection Bombardier Canadair
Regional Jet flying over Los Angeles, California

enhanced comfort, speed and distance.

SkyWest's Salt Lake City presence increased mightily in 1995 when the airline opened the 15-gate Concourse E in close proximity to Delta's operations.

1994
Two stock offerings held in one year.

1995
New Salt Lake City runway improved on-time performance and reduced fuel costs.

Four Delta Connection Regional Jets delivered, ten more ordered

In 1995, SkyWest tried improving its struggling California business, by carrying both Delta and Continental codes on some flights as this Bakersfield ad indicates.

THE REGIONAL JET: THE GREATEST TECHNOLOGICAL BREAKTHROUGH IN SKYWEST HISTORY

The Canadair Regional Jet (CRJ) allowed SkyWest to better serve outlying communities. The airlines defined these places as "long-haul, low-density" destinations. These cities were too far from hubs for turbo-props to reach, yet they had too little demand for full-sized jet service. The CRJs, powered by turbofan engines, traveled up to 530 miles per hour and could cover 1,700 miles without refueling. The significant impediment to their use—a clause in the United Airline pilots' contract limiting the number of jets a code-sharing regional could operate. In 2001, after modifications to that "scope clause," (thus named because it restricted the scope of regional carriers), SkyWest ordered 64 more regional jets.

Operated 115 daily flights from Los Angeles

Concourse E, 15 gates convenient to Delta gates, opened in Salt Lake City.

Entered into a code share alliance with Continental on all Los Angeles flights

Ron Reber appointed chief operating officer; Brad Rich became executive vice president

As **United Express,** SkyWest experienced

United Express Bombardier Canadair
Regional Jet flying over the Rockies.

record-breaking expansion.

After a quarter century, SkyWest touted its progress in this ad.

Each new Brasilia required an added 35 people. After becoming a United Express carrier in 1996, SkyWest engaged in a hiring frenzy adding 1,000 new employees – a 50% increase.

This photo of SkyWest Captain Earl B. Snow graced the cover of the company's 1997 Annual Report – 25 years after he flew the first Utah shuttle from St. George to Cedar City to Salt Lake City.

1996

1997

December:
Last Metroliner airplane retired

Adopted motto: "Working together to be the airline of choice"

Lee Atkin, Brent Atkin and Dell Stout retired from the board; Hyrum Smith, Henry Eyring joined the board.

> " It was out of necessity we did the United deal. When we decided to try it, I didn't think there was a chance in the world that it would actually work out. " — JERRY ATKIN

In 1997, SkyWest became a United Express carrier in 15 cities — Los Angeles, Burbank, Fresno, Imperial, Monterey, Ontario, Palm Springs, San Diego, Santa Barbara, San Luis Obispo, Santa Maria, and San Jose, California, plus Las Vegas, Nevada, Yuma, Arizona, and St. George, Utah. Twelve new stations opened in only 90 days — a remarkable feat.

SkyWest UNITED EXPRESS

Bigger. Better. More.

January: Became an all-cabin-class fleet

October: Signed agreement to become United Express carrier in 15 markets

In Los Angeles, SkyWest operated 120 daily United Express flights.

Celebrated 25th anniversary

Opened 12 new United Express cities in 90 days

SkyWest Country stretched from the Pacific

Seattle, Washington

Northwest to the Mississippi and beyond.

Memphis, Tennessee and
the Mississippi River

SkyWest Route Map 1998.

1998

SkyWest became
United's exclusive Express partner
on the West Coast

40 Brasilias
added to the fleet

San Francisco hub added

Expanded into
Pacific Northwest
as United Express

" Some companies look at **negotiation** as two parties bringing their needs to the table and then whittling at each other so everybody gives up something. We try to look at what everyone wants and see how we can work together to **make it all happen. "**

– JERRY ATKIN

SkyWest became an international carrier with Delta Connection flights from Salt Lake City, Utah, to Vancouver, British Columbia.

Fresno, California, the gateway to Yosemite National Park (above) and a longtime SkyWest Delta Connection destination, welcomed SkyWest United Express in 1997.

United Express service gave SkyWest passengers access to the Oregon Coast.

As United Express, SkyWest operated 84 daily flights from San Francisco.

Fresno, California, maintenance hangar opened

First international flight from Salt Lake City to Vancouver, B.C.

Portland, Oregon, maintenance hangar opened

In 2000, SkyWest Airlines was named top regional airline of the year by *Professional Pilot Magazine*. The April 2000 cover featured from left, SkyWest President Jerry Atkin, First Officer Tracey Ventresco, Captain Mike Nix, Flight Attendant Sonna Thigpen and Vice President of Flight Operations Brad Holt.

Chief Financial Officer Brad Rich supervised a public offering yielding more than $120 million.

Denver International Airport became SkyWest's sixth hub in 2001.

1999

Fleet included 99 aircraft.

Revenue up 45%.
Earnings up 100%.
Passenger count up 100%.

Named top regional airline
of the year by
Professional Pilot Magazine

2000

Named "Best Managed Regional Airline
in the World," by *Aviation Week and
Space Technology Magazine*

In September 2000, the first United Express Regional Jet was delivered.

Between September 11, 2001 and the end of that year, SkyWest added 20 new Regional Jets to its fleet. The Teton Mountains serve as a backdrop for this "RJ" and the Jackson Hole tarmac.

August Public Offering yielded $122.4 million.

Jets comprised 26% of the nation's regional fleet.

SkyShip service made it possible to track packages shipped via SkyWest Cargo.

Clause in United Airlines' pilots' contract restricted the number of jets regional airlines such as SkyWest could fly.

September: took delivery of first United Express regional jet

In 2001, the company's Salt Lake City Concourse E expanded to 28 gates and a state-of-the-art Salt Lake City maintenance hangar (shown at left) opened the same year.

Dallas, Texas, became SkyWest's seventh hub in 2001.

© Reuters NewMedia Inc./CORBIS

After September 11, 2001, increased security meant passengers were encouraged to arrive at airports two hours before their flights, and friends and family without tickets could no longer accompany passengers to gates.

2001

Delivery of 10 new regional jets

Salt Lake City Airport Concourse E expanded

Industry analysts touted SkyWest as "the universe's fastest growing regional."

Denver became SkyWest's sixth hub; Dallas became SkyWest's seventh hub.

DESTINATIONS

1992	✈ 42
1997	✈ 47
2001	✈ **90** cities in 23 states and Canada

PLANES

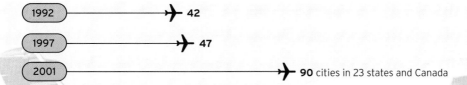

1992	✈ **48** – 19 Embraer Brasilias, 29 Metroliners
1997	✈ **53** – 10 Canadair Regional Jets, 43 Embraer Brasilias
2001	✈ **124** – 45 Canadair Regional Jets, 79 Embraer Brasilias

EMPLOYEES

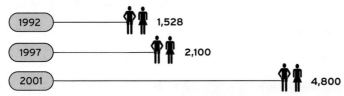

1992	1,528
1997	2,100
2001	4,800

PASSENGERS

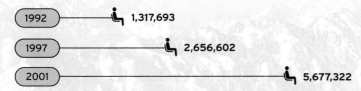

1992	1,317,693
1997	2,656,602
2001	5,677,322

September 15: Within five hours of an FAA all-clear signal, 75% of SkyWest's fleet was back in the air.

$2.6 million, 16,000 sq. ft. expansion of Palm Springs maintenance hub

September 11-14: Operations ceased as a result of terrorist-induced national tragedy.

November 13: Salt Lake City hangar open house

$4.7 million expansion of St. George headquarters

September 11, 2001 – terror took a toll on America. At the center of the crisis – commercial aviation. In the moments after the disaster, air traffic controllers, flight crews, and ground personnel landed 4,873 commercial aircraft with speed and efficiency. Airports stood vacant for four days. More than 130,000 flights were cancelled. On September 15, flights resumed with fanfare. A stunned nation rallied. Patriotism and solidarity swept the land and the airlines pondered complex solutions to unprecedented challenges.

"SkyWest's capability to weather this particular storm is not a matter of serendipity but the result of careful planning, commitment to performance, and a constant desire for achievement. These principles remain true for SkyWest people on an individual and collective basis."

–JERRY ATKIN

A desire for ever-increasing excellence:

THIS "CHARTERFEST" JET, PAINTED TO CELEBRATE SKYWEST AIRLINES' 30TH ANNIVERSARY, WAS PART OF A WHIRLWIND TOUR OF SKYWEST DESTINATIONS IN 2002. PICTURED AT LEFT WITH THE DENVER CREW.

SkyWest's secret for success.

2002 *and beyond*
THE FUTURE YEARS

In the months following the September 11, 2001 terrorist attacks, America slowly regained a sense of normalcy. SkyWest went about its business as always — adapting to circumstances. It opened a new hangar in Salt Lake City, worked through the renovation of its St. George headquarters, postponed plans for a Fresno expansion, opted to take delivery of more regional jets, and scrutinized how best to use resources.

In the midst of trying times, SkyWest found cause for guarded optimism with the year 2002. A fee-per-departure contract with Delta went into effect in January. The same month *Air Transport World* honored SkyWest as the regional carrier of the year for the second time. Salt Lake City, SkyWest's major hub, prepared to welcome its first Olympic Winter Games. Delta Airlines, a sponsor of the event, included SkyWest in plans to shuttle the Olympic Torch throughout the United States. Company representatives boarded a regional jet outfitted with a special Olympic paint job to carry the symbolic flame to Juneau and back — marking the first time the flame journeyed to Alaska.

During the Olympics, people from all over the world flew into Salt Lake City's airport. SkyWest's expanded concourse E was perpetually abuzz. The airline met the increased demand without a hitch.

Later in the year, in a marathon reminiscent of the torch relay, SkyWest took its 30th anniversary celebration to the skies. Another specially painted plane transported executives and employees on a whirlwind tour of SkyWest destinations. At every airport, outstanding employees were honored, and communities saluted. Above all, the airline continued to build relationships with the people and places it serves. It remained true to its primary goal — providing exceptional service to smaller communities.

As SkyWest concludes its third decade, America prepares to celebrate the centennial of the Wright Brothers first powered flight. That anniversary marks so much more than the launch of a boxy spruce bi-plane with muslin wings, and a four horsepower motor. Ever since Orville Wright managed a 12-second ride over a North Carolina sand dune, American aviation has been in a state of perpetual change. We, as a people, strive to go faster, farther, higher, and better. Airplanes help us achieve our dreams.

That won't change.

In the fast-paced world of aviation, a desire for ever-increasing excellence may be the only constant. This is one industry that can't stand still. The tragic events of September 11, hyper-intensified its evolution. In the aftermath of the most serious attack ever perpetrated against America, the only thing certain is that the future is unpredictable. SkyWest Airlines is not.

Throughout its history SkyWest has fine-tuned the art of adaptability. Its people combined unbridled optimism with tough financial discipline and a creative ability to solve problems. They worked hard to maintain a commitment to quality service, and made decisions based on a determination to "do the right thing." They sought opportunity when none seemed to exist. Those characteristics are indelible.

As the airline industry struggles to right itself, and hard economic realities come into play, air carriers that don't work efficiently may cease to exist. As efforts are made to consolidate resources, new relationships may emerge. Routes may be restructured, airports reconfigured, partnerships dissolved and new ones crafted.

Whatever the future, SkyWest Airlines remains, as always, up to the challenge. ✈

REGIONAL AIRLINE OF THE YEAR
2002
AIR TRANSPORT WORLD

SkyWest
A I R L I N E S ®

COMMEMORATIVE FLIGHT
2002 Olympic Torch Charter

BOARDING PASS

Regional Airline of the Year
SkyWest

Fire aboard airplanes is taboo – but when the flame fuels an Olympic torch special consideration is merited. Delta, the official airline of both the 1996 and 2002 Olympics, worked with FAA safety specialists and Georgia Tech' designers to create a bulk-head mounted lantern capable of securely transporting the flame across the ocean and around the nation. After winning the approval of the Department of Transportation, SkyWest's special Olympic Charter plane safely carried the apparatus and its torch to Alaska and back.

2002

SkyWest Airlines was named Regional Airline of the Year by *Air Transport World*.

SkyWest started aircraft dispatch school in St. George.

Tucson, Arizona maintenance facility opened

SkyWest became 100% contract or "fee for departure" carrier.

SkyWest Delta Connection Olympic Jet carried torch to Juneau, Alaska.

CharterFest – SkyWest raved about employees & destinations throughout the system

50th Regional Jet ordered

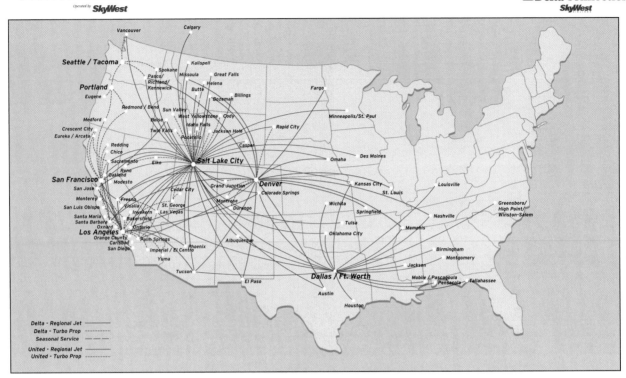

Route map, December 2002

2002 ✈ **93 destinations**

2002 ✈ **149 planes** – 73 Canadair Regional Jets and 76 Embraer Brasilias

2002 **5,000 employees**

2002 **Over 8 million passengers**

SkyWest's **inflight magazine** has grown to become
a beautiful communication tool between the airline, all the
communities SkyWest serves, and millions of
passengers traveling."

— ALISON GEMMELL, DIRECTOR OF SKYWEST'S PEOPLE DEPARTMENT

1982–1993

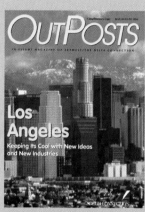

1994–1999

2000–Present

In December of 1999 the publication was fittingly re-named *SkyWest Magazine*. It continues to spotlight communities throughout "SkyWest Country". Entertaining and informative, the magazine captures the attention of passengers and provides them with an excellent way to bide their time. The reader gains knowledge about the awesome beauty, remarkable adventure, captivating history and incredible culture that SkyWest destinations offer.

SkyWest people *work hard to maintain*

25+ YEARS OF SERVICE EARL BLEAK SNOW ALAN KAY OLSON KLEN PARRY BROOKS JERRY C. ATKIN ANTHONY B. HOETKER CHARLES H. PITCHFORTH PATRICIA G. AVA LINDA BROWN

20+ YEARS OF SERVICE STEVEN D. BOVEE RONALD B. REBER ROGER K. ROSS MARC W. ANDRUS KEITH K.S. AVA RODNEY I. TAKAKI GINA MARIA RUSSO-HARTMAN PAMELA R. SNOW MARY K. SNOW KELLY MUMFORD JOSEPH B. RIMENSBERGER CAROL G. SORENSEN JOHN M. GORAL LARRAINE CALDWELL STACY H. FADDIS GARY M. GOODMAN ALDAN O. JUDD KEITH L. MALNAR MARY ELLEN CALL BIEBER GORDON MCKAY HEATON RALPH GERALD LEMON JEFFERY W. JACKSON LUPE ADAMS WILLIAM F. CLARK SANDRA C. GUTIERREZ ROBIN LEE WALL JAMES K. BOYD DOUGLAS A. LEE LELAND RAY VANCE ELIZABETH M. MAXWELL MARGARET G. AIKEN HARLAN L. MUNGE RICHARD A. RAMIREZ BRETT LELAND RUSHTON

15+ YEARS OF SERVICE BRAD LEE GALE TRACY ODELL MCCOY LORI LEI MALUFAU KO IELEMIA PIULA DEREK A. GREENAN JAMES H. SALLMON STEVEN F. DWIGGINS MICHAEL D. RENEHAN KENNETH B. ASHWORTH GARY A. MERKLEY C. PHILLIP ALFORD CHRISTY L. KELLER MARILYN A. LEKKERKERK NANCY L. RODRIGUEZ DAVID ALLEN KATSILAS ROBERT S. CLARKE BRADFORD R. HOLT ANDY D. OSTLER VICTORIA B. TARINELLI GARY D. HALL THOMAS ALAN KOUTZ MICHELE L. KATSILAS RONALD T. HOUSTON STEVEN PAUL SMITH JOEL RAY HINTZE JOSEPH G. CATANZARO JANICE STREET ANITA SPENCER JEFFERY DON BAILEY JIM KARL MILLER CHARLES A. WANLASS SCOTT J. MARTIN COLIN D. DUNCAN JACQUELINE A. PLATT ROBERT S. VENTURELLA MICHAEL D. HARTLINE JESUS I. VALOIS DEAN ALAN HEGER MARK S. SILVESTER STEPHEN RADFORD CREWS BENJAMIN H SOUTHLAND MARK B. BEEBOUT LAWRENCE R MOORE MICHAEL HADYKA LYNNITA L. MURPHEY ROBERT TROY RUSHTON SCOTT C. LAROCCO KATHRYN LORRAINE WURZBURG CHRIS OCONNR TORRES DEBORAH NUCKLES GREGORY D. HEATON WILLIAM MERL KELLOGG LAURIE KAY COX TAMRA THOMPSON SUSAN S. KELL L. DAVID STCLAIR EARLE R. DUMAS SHERYL L. PRICE JOHN W. BORLAND JOSEPH LITZ DONALD L. BEASLEY JIMMY J. ISOM GREG A. GRESZLER JIMMY A. LAMB DANNIE B. PAGE LONNIE COVINGTON TROY DWIGHT OLSEN THOMAS SABOL THOMAS E. SPEER BRENDA ANN SCATENA JUDI F. LEMON ELDON B. CORRY MARVIN DEAN TUBBS ALISON LEE GEMMELL JOHN BURK SHERI W. RHODES HOLLY D. BURNETT GAY A. BASTIAN LADAWN CHRISTENSEN MARY F. CONTI GILBERTO TORRES KARI FORD WELSH KATHRYN DIANA SYME ANTOINETTE OLSEN LORI A. HUNT CAROLYN R. POLAND ERIC D. CHRISTENSEN RENE Y. CORONADO BEN LESTER WATERS JOHN DAVID MORAN JOHN E. MINARDI GORDON P. HEWARD RULAN S. ADAMS STEPHEN T. WAYMAN JOHN DENNIS NEVE DONLEY E. WATKINS III STEVEN J. WATTIER KEVIN B. LAW LINDA S. LAUB PATRICIA W. FRYE JUAN M. PEREZ WENDELL K. SMITH JON R. TENPAS DEAN C. ENGLESTEAD BRUCE J. BALBIER MARK E. BUNKER MARIA PAPADAKIS GARY R. CHRISTOFFERSEN DAVID W. FADDIS JULIE A. BISHOP JANA O. GENTRY FARZAND ALI FARUKI JERRY W. PATTERSON LYNN KENT REDD JOSE M. FARFAN BRIAN A. WALLIMAN JONATHAN R. ORR DEL C BELYEA SANDRA L. KAPPEL EVERETT J. STRINGHAM JANA L. NIXON CAMIELLE ENCE DANIEL G. ENCE DENVER STRICKLING PAUL LESLIE STROLE JEFFERY L. WINKLER ALBERT Q. FORTUNATTI MICHAEL REED ALLSOP ESTRELLA A. AURE KEITH WILLIAM ADRIANCE JAMES H BREEZE DIANN H. JOHNSON RUSSELL TED STIENECKER MONT W. CAMPBELL JAMES J. MOONEY CLIFFORD W. CHANEY KATHRYN H. DEMARS CHARLES NAHOM PHILIP D. SUTHERLAND DONALD W. WILLIAMS DEVAN T. SHOPINSKI LYNN ERICKSEN INGMAR MUELLER ELIZABETH A. BETTER JAMES E. HEALEY ERIK Z. LEE WILLIAM F. LINDSAY ROBIN FAUCHER OSBORNE DAVID A. OWEN DIXIE COOPER KIMBERLE D. WISE-NELSON ROBERT W. BUNNELL KATHERINE A. CUSHING

10+ YEARS OF SERVICE PATRICK R. EVANS JENNIFER FORAYTER KELVIN B. ADAMSON WILLIAM L. PIGOTT DAVID W. HESSER NECIA G. CLARK-MANTLE JULIE A. AGAPINAN BRIAN L. ALLDREDGE ARTHUR B. EMERY RANDY L. STRATE GEORGE M. PERKINS JAMES WARREN BYBEE DARRELL G. COOK PETER E. ENSTROM DAVID OOSTRA THOMAS M BARDEN SAN GELINAS JOHN STEVENS MICHAEL R. KOHLMEYER RUTH MARY LAWRENCE MITCHELL H. LUCAS JOSEPH ANTONELLI LATRICIA GLEED DAVID M. BANDLI MICHAEL J. BERRY BRADFORD R. PETERSON SHEREE ANN ADAMS JEFFREY L. JONES BRETT R. MORGAN JAMES S. CARSON RONAN ALAN NORTE MICHAEL MUMFORD CARL CURTIS SIX DON B. RICH BRIAN KEITH SWIFT KIMBERLEY A. BRADSHAW VINCE A. ORNELAS ERIC M. FROST BRADFORD R. RICH DONNA A. WHITE MARIANNE L. BASINGER SUSAN CHRISTENSEN JULI JONES KEMET R. BABCOCK RICARDO FRAGOSO TOM LESTER JEFFRIES DIRK J. OLSON LA VERNE WALTON JIMMIE D. MORGAN HERMAN MICHAEL GIBSON SCOTT L. WATERS RONDA BROWN D. BRENT HENRIE STEVEN L. HART LEROY K. LOFTIS GARY OVERBAUGH DAVID J. BECHTOLD THOMAS E. COOK MARK ERIC GRANT JERRY T. ROSE MICHELLE L. NEWELL JOANNE B. FERGUSON STEVEN C. MATTHEWS RILEY P. JACKSON BRYAN C. GAMBLES MICHAEL L. CAPPS JOE M. SANCHEZ MICHAEL E. EISENSTAT MARK RONALD SORENSEN TRACI K. FITZGERALD RODOLFO CASTANEDA STEVEN L. BAXTER DEBRA ANN SCHWENKE GARY R. GREEN LORI L. DAVIS HEIDI M. BOWDEN BRUCE A. BRADFORD SAMUEL D. TERRY PAUL B. ACCORDINO BRUCE W. BARCLAY C. BLAINE WALSH BRETT H. DETWILER GRANVILLE C. FENTON DANIEL F. SHARP SHAWN CHRISTY VANCE DARRYL KAY CHRISTIAN PAUL WESLEY CLARK NICHOLAS R. PELLEGRINO BYRON F. GBASSAGEE MARAIJA J. FINUCANE DEBORAH M. ABAD BRIGITTE M. ANDRESEN REBECCA ANN GRIFFITH EVANTHEA J. KORDOPATIS BRADLEY C. SMITH WAYNE LEWIS DAVIES WAYNE EMIL KOMAREK SCOTT G. TAYLOR STEPHANIE L. HERRERA MATTHEW T. SHEPHERD ALBERT BELL BLOSCH STEPHEN M. ANDERSON ROBERT A. FETCHIN WILLIAM O. LANHAM GARRY C. POULTON TIM R. SCHAEFER WILLIAM SCHLUETER LYNN ARTHUR HOLYOAK STEVEN O. SHELLEY JOHN J. LABER III RICHARD E. BOYCE BRENT CLARK DONALD SMITH DOUGLAS SUZANNE F. GARRETT PETER G. WAGSTAFF ALDEN ALLAN ELIASON HENRY C. GEREN EMILY K. BECHTOLD KAREN G. HOEFER WAYNE D. WIGNALL DEBRA S. GUENTHER JACK RENTINK JACK RICHARD ALEXANDER STEVEN CHRIS CARSON JESUS A. LOPEZ DARREN W. MOYES FRANCES D. TRUJILLO DIANA LYNNE FETTERS RALPH L. SHARTZER BILL C. DYKES NANCY H. TAYLOR LAUREN KIM ENCE LISA M. KIRKPATRICK HARLEY E. GRIGGS FRANK P. POPP DANIEL H. STILES JEFFREY A. LISKE GUY DANTON WETZEL HIRAM M. DRANE MARK STEVEN HARTENSTINE GERALD L. PENNINGTON RAY CRAWFORD BENNETT ANTHONY L. WOOD CONNIE Y. ADAMS ANDY J. HOWELL ANNETTE M. STETTLER GARY BRUCE ANDERSON RICHARD J. MUELLER JR. CONNIE S. MCCLASKEY LISA ANN SMITH KATHY JO HERD BOBBI C. SEVY JAMES BRIAN JENSEN ERIC HALL BAARDSETH JAMES M. BRINK CANDY C. CURTIS-HO STEPHEN G. KANUCH JERRY C. SMITH HARMON ALLEN BELKNAP PATRICIA ANN JARABA SHELLI H. GARCIA JONATHAN K. GRAFF KELVIN L. HYATT CLAY K. VAN ETTEN WALLACE E. COLSON PHILLIP M. ANTHONY MARK B. THOMAS DANIEL J. HERMAN MICHAEL E. OWIECKI DAVID M. KESSELMAN WILLIAM W. PARRISH CHRISTOPHER DIRK PRATT KELLY CYRUS STEVENS DONALD PYLE GRAHAM SUSAN ELAINE CLOUD JAMES A. THOMPSON JON ROBERT FISHER KRISTINA MARIE WYATT FRANKLYN FREDERICKSEN CAROL GONZALEZ RANDY T. CHAPPELL ALAN B. FREDERICK BENJAMIN J. SMITH JANICE A. KIVISTO DOUGLAS A. FORD MARK S. KOTEK THOMAS E. MACFARLANE CHARLES W. PAYTON EDWARD PAUL RUBOTTOM SCOTT T. SOLUM NATALIE DAYTON BUNKER R. RUSSELL BENNETT GARY W. BISHOP MARTIN W. FARMER DAVID MARK RASMUSSEN JEFFREY A. SCHROEDER MICHAEL R. SPURGEON MARK THOMAS WEIGEL SHEN RAJAN PAMELA WANGENSTEEN PATSY R. REYNOLDS TERRY M. VAIS KAYLIN V. COLEMAN JILL C. JENKINS SHERRI HAN PATTON MARIA N. MARTINEZ KAYE ANN PHALON MARIE WELCH ROBERT M. TOPLIFF CHARLES D. CUSHING CHRISTOPHER BEAR DANIEL ROSS BLACK MICHAEL LEE BREWSTER BRUCE G. TAYLOR YORK N. ZENTNER ROWENA D. YAPIT ERIC D. NELSON KAREN B. GALLAGHER REGINA RACHELLE BACON MAKAY O. CAMPBELL CRISTINA HERNANDEZ BRANDEE BLACK NICHOLAS P. CATANESE RICHARD W. DOMONDON GABRIELA E. RODRIGUEZ CLAIRE PADRON TOMAS N. GALLEGO KELLIE GREENELSH BEN EARL MCCOY PAULA ANNE MACAYA TERRANCE L. PAYNE ANDREA LEA LANTHIER JULIE ANN ANDRADE JEANETTE GILLMAN MICHELLE J. MEUWISSEN ALPHA ILEENE WENDLAND KIM E. FALCO KIM MICKALA BOWN DANIEL T. GILES DAVID D. MAJEWSKI SHAUN R. SHATTUCK DOUGLAS A. AMBROSE CLINTON V GODFREY FALEASIU TAFITI JOAO BOSCO L COSTA LEDDY TREFFRY CURTIS SHANETTE VV BROOKS JOSEPH H. FULLER JOSEPH S. SIGG PAMELA S. CLARK LAURA K. MCCONAHY FRANKLIN J. ANDREWS JAMES BLACK SCOTT A. CARR PETER EDWARD CASIL ROY W. GLASSEY JR. BRIAN A. GRAY JAMES D. GUNDERSON JR. PAUL W. JENSEN GREGG P. SORENSEN JOHN N. WANGENSTEEN CHRISTINE WONG-CERVANTES WILLIAM A. KELLY JACK DUANE MELTON GRETE H. WRIGHT KYLE C. HOWES JACK V. LEONIS THOMAS S. LAMB CARRIE A. PING JOSE LUIS LIMON BLAIR C. PETERSON CARMEN L. CAPITO JR. EDWARD TROY PEARMAIN CHRISTINE M. MYERS STEPHANIE A. DOTY LORRAINE ALLSOP JULI LISH IOANE M. NAUTU BRENT G. MULLINS JOHN D. SYME MICHAEL J. KRAUPP. BENNETT P. CRAWFORD GARTH S. BLACK AMY M. QUINN SUSAN HILL HOWEY SHARON M. COLSON KEITH E. PARRISH MICHELLE LEE BROUGH DAVID E. VAUGHN MYRNA MARIE BEITNER JAMES JOSEPH SKEAHAN GARY HAROLD LIST DARREN C. MCCLISH JULIE ANNE WILLIAMS BRENT L. WILSON STACY AMELIA SINE

5+ YEARS OF SERVICE HENDRIKS K. KAPOH TERESA ANN SHOPE ANTHIA R. ASHE SHANE LOSEE ROBIN L. MYERS ALMA DELOIS WALKER HAROLD ALLEN JR. MARILYN L. KASTER BARBARA M. LUDWIG JACK ALLEN SHRADER ALLAN LYMAN WEINER J. PHILLIP HADDEN BRAULIO CHACON JANE OSBORN MARIA OLIVIA ALMEIDA KEITH R. FROST LEW B. BODKIN JOHN CHARLES FLEMING JOAN TOMSETT-SMITH CYNTHIA LEAVITT MOLIS MICHAEL E. SORENSEN ELIZABETH ENCARNACION ESTER M. FUNGLADDA GREGORY NOVAK SHERMAN D. GRIM LANA J. STEWART JEFFREY L. ARENSON JOSEPH E. JAMES STEPHANIE A. JARDINE CHARISSE HUTCHINGS ANNE M. SAWTELLE MARIA JAMES JOY DENISE MARTINEZ MICHELE SHATTUCK SUZIE A. SMITH ROBERT

the highest quality service and safety.

DAVID RICE KENNETH R. TALLEY DONYA GAYLE JOHNSON CARLA LEE REINKE WENDY ADAMS JAMIE MARY BERRY STEPHEN E. MARINO MARK L. GANNON CHAD L. HOLLINGWORTH MAX PATRICK PARKER GILBERT ROMERO ROBERT M. JARDINE HENNA BROWN KEVIN J. MATTHEWS ROY ALMEIDA MICHAEL J. SPEARS SUZANNE L. STEPHENSEN NICOLE PINNEO JANINE KOTEK KATHERINE D. KILLIAN DOLORES S LETO WENDY D. PRIDDY ANJA B D ROMERO DARLENE MORRISON MICHAEL J SPENCER GLORIA S. ALDRICH LORI MARIE KOLLER JAMES H. SCHERFFIUS JOHN M. STENGER BRANDON ERMINI DEAN GARY VANDEBRAKE JOHN ELLIS WIEBE C. MARGO PINEDA JULIA M. DAVIS BRIAN MORTENSON DAVID BRENT OMER HEATHER M. ROGERS ANITA LOUISE BUTTERFIELD MICHELLE A. LOTT DAVID S. HINCKLEY JILL MARIE OMAN CRYSTAL D. SUDOL JENNY L. NICOLAY JULIE DEANN LOVE KATHLEEN A. MOORE SHIRLEY ADDY DANIEL G. DEHAAN MARIE EL-SAYED GENOVEVA ALEXANDRA HEINZ EDNA MOLINA ESTHER J MONTIEL SALWA MUKLASHY JOHN R. GALLADORA WILLIAM E. HEITMEIER PAUL W. LESTER TERRY DON RIEDEL BEN PALMER KAYLYNN GREBSTAD LORI LYNN GRUENWALD BRETT E. WHITE MARIA J. RYKS DONOVAN B. JOHNSON ERNIE NEBIT PENNY A. THAETE ALTON GEAN BURGETT JOSEPH ROHNER EDWARD V. FOWLES MICHAEL L. GRIGGS LESLIE W. MCCLURE LYNDA LEE GREEN ANNE W. PIKULA KARIN E PETERSON GABRIELLE GERRITS-PORTER CRAIG R. LAYTON EVAN LYLE BECK TRACY T. GALLO ERIC J. MICHELSON DANIEL R. VALENTINI ANDREW BAIRD ZINK DEBORAH S. RUSSELL MICHAEL J. STAHL RALPH PAUL WYMAN TUONG NGUYEN TRISHA CHAMNESS SUSAN K. COX RACHEL BEALL BLANCHARD BARBARA ANNE KARR BRANDON MUNRO LISA DEAN CONNIE E. OLSON AARON B. BUTTARS LORNA MILLER-JOHNSON CRYSTAL SMITH JEFFREY A. TANNER GARY GIESSEN KEVIN M. JENSEN JAY W. BEHRENS OLGA MARIA CABRERA LANCE E. LUBICK CONNIE C. SILVA RAYMOND E. WAGNER JOLENE K. WARNER TROY L. WITHERS ELI ANTHONY BORTOLAZZO FRANCES M. PRENTIS ERNIE REYES TORRES JAVIER RECALDE JOHN A. WEATHERBURN AMY L. JONES SUMENS JAMES E. BIXBY FRANK ELDRIDGE HAMMOND MICHAELYN M. CURTIS MATTHEW A. NACKOS MICHAEL SANCHEZ KATHLEEN D. BRYAN CYDNEY MARSHALL BRACKEN LINDA C. JACKSON CHELTA WILDE ALLRED ARTURO NOE MARTINEZ EDWARD S. RICO ALEX FITZGERALD KIRK D. HUNSAKER EDWARD A. ROY GERALD THOMSON JON C. PARKINSON NADINE ZIEGLER KATHRYN A. LARKIN SHANE MURPHY JAMES B. OSMENT MARTIJN SAMSOM KELLY BROOK POTTER TODD P. SCHREIER GLENN H. KARDOL JAMES F. KELLY MARTHA JEAN RAPOLLA SHARON J. GLEED ALICE R. STOHL MARQUITA GAIL MCKEE DOREEN MAULDING CONNIE FINGER JAMES M. KELLY MICHAEL K. FINCH THOMAS E. GRATTON KEVIN A. LEAVITT LISA MARIE ROUMPOS DENNIS LYNN RINEHART JILL N.F. AYLOR ROGER C. COSTA WAHIDULLAH DADGAR ANTHONY FIZER STEVE F. JOHANSEN TODD MILLER WELLS GREGORY J. WOOD LUIS ESTALA JR. BRADLEY R. FORD JAIME LUE SORENSEN SIAOSI A. FITISEMANU CHRISTINE MERRILL TODD S. ST. THOMAS TRACI FLYNT VANGELDER ROBIN COLMENERO JOSEPH M. CABLE MELANEE MICHELLE MONSEN CURTIS REID CHILD ROBERT HUDSON CONNIE CHRISTENSEN HARRIS SCOTT E. MILLER SAGHAR MARIA MASOUMEH PEYVANDI MICHELE ANDREA REID JUSTIN R. SHEA KAREN M. RUZICKA NIKKI LYN VEJNAR ANTHONY D. THOMPSON ALI KOOCHAKI DAVID HOWARD LARSEN ROBERT D. LINCOLN RAYMOND H. MOORE PAUL S. PHILLIPS HERBERT F. SOHN JR. GIUSEPPE MARZOCCA ANTHONY L. JACOBS GEORGE W. MARSHALL ANABELL PORRAS DAVID R. WHITTAKER CYNTHIA PU RONALD DEAN SIMONS JR. CARLOS A. LOPEZ ROBERT L. SURONEN BRUCE L. ERICKSEN CURTIS R. SESSIONS HUGO ANIBAL ALARCON ROBERT SHAN THOMAS KRISTINA M. SOLI JENNIFER L. HODGES KAY LYNN NELSON PATRICIA B. MITCHELL DANIEL P. JARVIS TERRY DEAN STEED NICOLE DRAAYER ASHTON JARED AFUALO MARC R. CAMPBELL JOHN W. KEMP CHRISTOPHER DAVID ABELL THOMAS R. CALDWELL MICHELE DILLON THOMAS P. HIMKA BARBARA ANN PUGMIRE CODY M. CROSBY JOHN D. BLANCHARD MISTY D. JOHNSTON LARENA A. BEAL CHRISTINA MICOL SOHN MILAN JANCOVIC DARREN S. FRODSHAM BOYD D. JOHNSON CAROL PETERSON JAMES A. CARLSON SCOTT OREN STEPHENS BRYAN M. STOUT MARCUS L. KELLY CHRISTI L. CARPENTER DERRICK Q. JUDD WESLEY WAYNE MATTHEWS BRYAN G. PEACOCK BRAD EARL SHEEHAN JAIME A. MANRIQUE PETER GORAN BLOMQUIST ENRIQUE D. TOMAS DONALD RILEY DANIELSON SCOTT EDWARD JENSE TRACIE L. FERNANDEZ STEPHEN R. MALLOW OSEAS IRA ADUNA JR LEWIS P. BJORK MATTHEW J CASEY EDNA MOSQUERA SUSAN DELIA ARRINGTON GARY BRIAN HUGHES SALLY OJA RICHARD EDWIN WATSON BRYAN LEYSTRA ELAINE C. WOLFF GARY R. CLASEN NATHAN KLOSTER ANDREW K. BRATTINI TAMARA R. DIAMOND NATALIE L. WARNER KAREN A. FISHER GUY M HAWKINS BRYAN JAY ANDERSON FRANCINE M. COX SONYA WOLFORD WENDY BORG DAVID A. BOTTINELLI BRIAN L. MARION DAVID EVAN HYLLESTED LESLIE MARK EDWARDS BARRY MARK GORMAN ALBERTO NEGRON MARK A. WENDEL JOSHUA D. LEAVITT FRANCIS LOPEZ JANA FISHER ANDERSON TIMOTHY L. BRAUN DAVID B. TATE ALAN F. ANDERSON MICHAEL D MURRAY GLENN G. CAPRON RYAN D DOWNS TONY HUITRON EMANUEL FAYE M. WILSON TIMOTHY JENNINGS JONATHAN FRANKS WENDY M. PETERSON JONATHAN PIERCE TUFI ANNE NAEA WILLIAM MOORE MAJOR RAYMOND JEFFREY P. GARN ROBERT GRASER TIMOTHY R. LAWLER TITUS J. MCDANIEL DARYL VON MEANS YESSI HOLBROOK JANICE L. HOOVER WILLIAM H. JEFFERIES CHARLES F. BARBER SONDRA HELEN ZERNIS KIMBERLY R. LESKO LINDA RHODES HARVEY R. LAYTON BEN L. RACICOT LARRAINE H. VAN ORDEN TANYA CHOJNACKY PAMELA ANN MCDANIELS TARA BOYER MATHESON DAVID LORNE PAXMAN LAWRENCE D. LARUE TEDDI M. VAIL KATHRYN L. OMER DARRELL LEON COOK ANTHONY AGNEW JOHN T. BELL KANDI ANN COLEMAN JENNIFER A. REYES MARK S. LEKIC OLIVER J. LEAVITT KEITH DARREL LONG BLADE GREENWOOD KEITH M. MCRAE JOSEPH D. PFEIFFER LEISL ANNE LEYSTRA KATHY DENISE JACKETTA KATHRINE F. MAKASIAN JUDITH C. SNYDER DERRICK E. DEARDEN ANITA MANTHEI THOMAS D'AMICO BRYAN R STALTER NANCY ANN HICKMAN ERIK KEITH MYLI JERI LYN LIDDIARD ANGALEE D. SWENSON SHAWN LELAND HUDSON SHARON THOMAS TRACEY N. THOMAS CHRISTOPHER BAUMGARTNER ROBIN DEE MILLER LEIF W. ABOTNES CHRISTIAN B. EYRING ROBERT L. KIBLER DEREK PAUL PRATTE LOUIE C RODRIGUEZ BRIAN A. NUSS JANICE B. OLIVER ERIK M. FRENCH PATRICK J. GORMLEY WILLIAM GEORGE HILL III DEBRA JANE CARROLL KATHLEEN M. DAVIS CHRISTY L. EASTMAN TIFFANY D. TAYLOR MELVA L. DUNBAR CONNIE JOLLEY SHELLIE R. CHAPMAN MANUEL O. AGUILAR THOMAS J. BERAZ TRENA LEFEVRE KARINA F. ANDREASEN BILL E. BURGETT JEREMY E. LEAVITT CHARLES TIMOTHY BUTLER MARVIN R. PETERSEN KEELEY DIXSON BRANDI G. HONEY MARK ALLEN CHILDRESS TRACY D. SMITH SHERI LOUISE PAULSEN LAUREL JOAN HIRZEL YARET JIMENEZ PATRICIA REED TAMRA WOODLAND DENISE L. KEIPER ROBERT P. JONES CLIFTON S. OKAMOTO PER H. SOLBERG JACQUELINE R. NIELSEN MARLA MCDONALD HEIDI I. WILSON MICHAEL E. NEWMAN IPUSILIVA A. FAFAI LARRY J. PADILLA CATHERINE ESTHER DIX GEORGIA LEE ROYLE ELLEN T. STERN STACY MARIE RUSSELL CHARLES DEJESUS KATHY LYNN CHATWIN LUIS AVEYTUA GREGORY A. DONLIN BILL T. MOSTOWY MICHAEL J. PEART MICHAEL R. KASE AMY LYNN RASMUSSEN MATTHEW D. GOODRICH LUKE LYDEN SONDRA JETTY HANEY KIMBERLY K. IRENE GWENDOLYN KRUGLE JUDIE PATTON BRYAN KELLY DOMER BO ATKINS CHERYL E. KVENVOLD HEATHER RACHEL BIDLEMAN MICHAEL E. BRONSON DANIEL L. SCHWAB NORMA ALEJANDRA AGUILAR NOREEN L. LLANDERAL ROBERT MORALES PHALLY PING FRANCISCO J. VELASQUEZ JOLE A. SCHIFFER KRISTIN MARIE AHLSTEDT JILL A. BAKER LARALEE HERZOG MELISSA S. OWENS DONALD S. SCHMID JR. RICHARD LAMOINE LOVE GREGORY M. BURTON TODD J. CHURCH JAMES G. DEFARGES JOHN KOPAUNIK MALIA A. SELE JAMES ROBERT KING TRINKA MADSON KIMBERLY A. SECHREST DONNA M. GRAY JAMES E. COCHRANE DAVID G. WEST WILLIAM A. DAVIS ANDREW RAUL CANIDATE POLLY PRINCE HOUSLE TONY HERRON MYRON P. GROVES JR. SHAWNA M. OVARD BRIAN H. KAMM MARK D. KELLEY HARRY TORONIANS DANETTE THOMPSON KIMBERLEE E. BIDLE JEREMIE LINGLET KARI MENDICINO THERESA REYES PANGELINAN WAYNE D. ROSIER JAMES L. ADAMS WILLIAM L. BOICE KURT H. CHRISTIANSEN TODD A. CLAUSEN KENNETH S. COBB KELLY LASSITER ANDREW LEYVA RONALD G. RAMIREZ CHRISTIAN R. RIPPE JASON BRADY STATHAM ANNELIESE RENE TOMLINSON MIKE E. ZIMMER CHRISTOPHER ARNOLD CHERIE K. SCHLEICHER DAVID A. FORD GABRIELA N. LICEA CHARESE LYNA MILLER KIANA BAIR BRADLEY W. BLAKE JENNIE DORA RODRIGUEZ JOE D. ORTIZ JESUS J. SALAZAR RICKY D. WYMER GREG J. RUNGE RONALD JAMES DAHLQUIST JIM WOODARD SCOTT J. COWLEY MARK HUSS SHAWN P. MAI THOMAS SCOTT ROBBINS JULIE KAY CURTIS JOHN D. LINNEBUR DONALD W. ENGER DARREN LEE HOWELL TRACIE ANNE BRYANT ANGELICA K. WALLACE CARLOS BLANSKI JEANETTE A. HOVEY RUSSELL S. KRAUS DAVID M. STANDING SHERI IVY BAKER DENA K. BINGHAM RENEE SHAFTER AMEE SWENSON YOUNG KERRY CLARK HUTCHINGS TIMOTE C. VAMANRAV JACOBINE CLOUD MARGARET MARIE TOILOLO EDWARD D. BERRY CHERYL ANN KOPOIAN MATTHEW FRED ORTEGA JESUS PLASCENCIA DONCARLOS BATEMAN NELLY HERNANDEZ ELISA GREENLAW KATHLEEN L. COLBY DIANE JAMESON KARALEE HEINER SMITH JASON D. CALDWELL SUE ELLA MONREAL NATHAN ALEXANDER GUSTAVO CHAVEZ STACI A. CORGAN MICHIHARU ISHITANI ERIC HENSLEE PAUL L. VONSEGGERN FILIP BROOS DAVID W. GLINES RUBY WALTHALL NORMA V. ANDRADE KIMBERLY K. MIDDLETON NADINE B. YOUNG ROMEAD KAUTTO NEILSON DENISE LYNETTE LINCOLN OTIS B. ALLEN KENDRA L. KEY CHRISTINE A. SEVERIN RAMIRO GOMEZ JR. AMY E. BLANCO LISA ROWE SILVINO T. PERALTA WAYNE DWIGHT WATSON JOSEPH MC CORMACK JURATE SEPUTYTE WILLIAM WARREN MELANIE LEATHAM JACQUELINE GRACIA JAMIE C. TARRANT JOHN GARY BELIN MYRON J. BOOKER JORGE CAMARENA WILLIAM CURTISS RUSSELL C. DRUETT JAMES E. SIMS ORLANDO ALFONSO OTIS HEATH EDWIN HERNANDEZ KWESI JOHNSON FRANCISCO MUNOZ PETER RAMSEIER HOWARD JAY FRANK CHERYL C. VIRAMONTES SANTOS A. ARRIOLA MARCUS LEE BUTLER DAMON FOWLER LAMAR JOHNSON JR. STEVEN MOLINA ROBERT W. MOYER JOSE LUIS RAMIREZ JUAN RUELAS GRADY J. SIMS CHRISTOPHER SMITH SAMUEL VALENCIANO RICARDO H. VEGA VICTOR TRIEN WONG RENAN TOMAS ERIC D. JONES ROBERT S. WILLIAMS LYNNE G. RAWLINGS KEITH ALLEN RITARI PETER CHRISTIAN BUTLER EDUARDA MARIA CHAVEZ JOEL BELTRAN CORPUS HYDIE M. SWEET YOLANDA VILLEGAS PRUDHUME RODEL C. RUTAQUIO ANITA KAUR JOHANSSON ANGELA RIVERA TYLER CRISPIN STACIE DAWN GIBSON SANDRA MOORE DAY JESSICA ANNA LEONIS CAROLINA FRANCIS STACEY JONES DAVID H. HEIDEMANN JAMES GARNER ROBERTO JOSE ARAUZ SCOTT C. DEWAR ALMA C. SMITH MARIA D. SYLVESTER STEVEN L. LESASSIER MAUREEN RUSS LYNN G. JOHNSON FREDERICK D. THOMAS JASON D. BURGESS HENA MELY RODRIGUEZ ROSARIO A ROMERO

ALLIES IN ACHIEVEMENT

BY DIANE RONAYNE

No company **succeeds** solely on its own.

Throughout
its colorful history SkyWest Airlines consistently recognized that business relationships are "people" relationships. The same principles of integrity and fairness that characterizes the airline's corporate culture have traditionally applied to its business dealings. As a result, SkyWest has benefited from positive associations with many other entities—from food service vendors to aircraft suppliers, to cities and their airports. These allies own a share in SkyWest's achievement. Their equally intriguing stories follow.

EMBRAER

The best word to describe the relationship between Embraer, the world's fourth-largest manufacturer of commercial airplanes, and SkyWest Airlines, is "symbiotic." Embraer is not just a vendor, not simply providing customer service. And SkyWest is something more than a customer—more like a friend.

For one thing, the western regional representative for Embraer lives in Salt Lake City. For 13 years, Fred Reina has been the consistent, dependable human interface between the two companies, interacting with both on a daily basis from his office located in the SkyWest facility.

For another, as Fred recalls, SkyWest was there for Embraer at a time—soon after the Gulf War in 1993, when the whole aviation industry was shuddering—when it really meant something.

It all began in 1985, when SkyWest placed its first order with Embraer, then owned by the government of Brazil. The plane SkyWest wanted,

A SkyWest airliner in production

the EMB120 Brasilia, was a 30-seat turbo-prop model. It beat out its competition for the contract because it could fly efficiently "hot and high"—in and out of high-altitude airports with high average annual temperatures. These airports typified those served by the young western regional airline based at 2,880-foot St. George, Utah.

SkyWest liked the first 30 EMB120s so much that in 1993 the company went back to Embraer to order 20 more. That's when the symbiosis really began.

"SkyWest was doing so well that they decided to place another order with us," Reina recalls. "That was a big, big shot in the arm for us. In 1993, Embraer was on the verge of financial devastation. We and the whole aviation industry were in difficult times. We had a problem. We could build the planes but could not supply the engines or avionics because we didn't have money to

pre-purchase them for our customers' airplanes. That was quite devastating for us. We were even laying people off. Then SkyWest stepped in and prepaid for the engines and avionics, so the manufacturers would ship them to us, so we could make the planes."

This kind of situation was almost unheard of, Reina said. "It would be like someone going into a dealership to buy a car and having the dealer tell them he could sell them a car, but it wouldn't have an engine in it because the dealer couldn't afford it. Then having the dealer ask the buyer to prepay him for the engine so he could complete the sale and the buyer saying, 'Sure, I'll be glad to.'"

When SkyWest stepped up to the plate, the company demonstrated a high level of trust. "SkyWest had confidence in Embraer," Reina said. "They were making a lot of money with this airplane so they wanted more. When airlines buy airplanes, they buy them because they have set up future route structures, are projecting passenger loads, have more cities to fly to, and so they need more planes. That was happening in 1993 when SkyWest placed that order."

In 1997, business was booming for SkyWest,

The EMB120 Brasilia

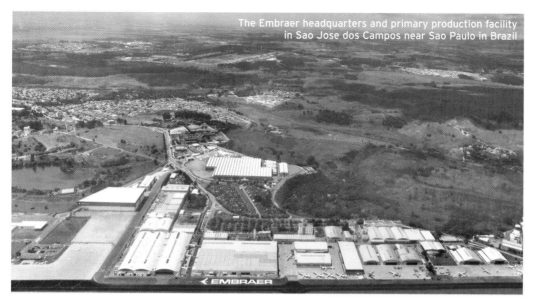

and the company began to increase the number of EMB120s it flew. Purchasing used Brasilias all over the world, SkyWest eventually flew 92 of the efficient turboprops. "That is a huge number of just one model to maintain," Reina says, "but they really like that plane. Right now, with 80 in the air, SkyWest is the largest Brasilia operator in the world and will remain so through 2005, with a projected stable of 50."

SkyWest also has the distinction of flying the Brasilia with the highest hours and flight cycle record in the world. Plane number N186SW has more than 46,000 take-off/landing cycles under its belt, which calculates out to more than 38,000 hours logged. Again using an automobile analogy, it would be comparable to a one-owner car that had been babied since it was brought home 200,000 miles ago.

"To look at this plane and see that many hours and cycles on it, you'd think you wouldn't want it," Reina says. "Fortunately, SkyWest probably has the best maintenance program in the whole industry. This particular airplane is really a good airplane because it has been maintained so well."

Although there will always be markets best suited for the EMB turboprop family of airplanes, Embraer moved ahead in the 1990s to design and build aircraft for the commercial regional jet market. There Embraer has created a fine track record with its ERJ family of 37-seat, 44-seat and 50-seat jetliners. In fact, the ERJ145 50-seat regional jet is the most advanced and profitable jetliner in the commuter market worldwide. Through June 30, 2002, a total of 577 firm orders for the ERJ145 have been received, 428 have been delivered, and 314 additional purchase options have been entered in ERJ145 sales order logbooks.

Its newest sibling, the extra long-range ERJ 145XR, offers a 2,000 nautical mile range, significantly longer than other commercial regional jets in the 50-seat class, as well as improved hot-and-high operation capabilities and superior single engine ceiling. Equipped with winglets that give measurably reduced specific fuel consumption, the ERJ145XR introduced significant improvements on design weight characteristics of the basic airframe and increased capacity fuel cells. Following its successful first flight, in July 2001, the model entered the certification process, and is expected to be in service by the end of 2002.

The ERJ145

The future for Embraer lies in filling the gap currently existing between 50-seat regional jets and 120-seat airliners, Reina explains. "Several companies are developing a new family of jets to fill it. We have the EMBRAER 170 family of airplanes in flight test now. Swiss (formerly SwissAir) is lined up as our first European customer. Leasing company GECAS and several other European carriers have all placed orders for this new family."

What's driving this move to mid-size jets? "The major airlines are not doing very well since 9/11," Reina observes, "and they may be looking at smaller airplanes sized perfectly for the routes they're flying and the loads they're getting. At the same time, regional airlines like SkyWest are doing more flying on longer routes for their major airline partners and are therefore looking at moving up into a larger airplane. The new EMBRAER 170 family is designed for this market."

Logic might suggest that airlines should simply remove seats from larger planes to solve the problem of shrinking passenger loads, but Reina says that would be a mistake. "Much of the cost of operations of a plane is related to its size, weight and fuel consumption, as well as the number of seats on board. The answer is to design an aircraft specifically for this new marketplace. You can't just take seats out of a big plane in order to serve a regional market. It's not cost-effective." Most experts see the potential for $200 billion in mid-size aircraft sales for the regional jet market, he adds. "It's huge—the fastest-growing segment of air travel."

It's an exciting, scary time for the air travel industry as a whole, Reina notes—for airline suppliers, airplane manufacturers and passengers

as well. In this era of great change, SkyWest is well positioned for success.

"SkyWest is a perfect example of an airline that provides service to cities the big airlines wouldn't come to, and does it with planes sized for the market in terms of seats and performance," Reina points out. "Some airports can't support large planes or their short landing strips require a turboprop. If we are going to maintain the level of service to communities around the country that is critical to their development, we have to have air travel. And the major airlines will continue to support the regional carriers. To get from Boise, Idaho, to Paris, France, you need a way to reach the major airline's hub, so the major carriers will rely more and more on regional affiliates to feed passengers to them and continue to spur their economic growth."

Diversification of product and creating symbiotic relationships have marked Embraer's progress from its founding as a state-owned company in 1969, through its privatization in 1994, and beyond. Today, the company circles the globe, employing almost 12,000 people in its Sao Paulo, Brazil, headquarters and subsidiaries, offices and customer services bases in the United States, France, Australia, China and Singapore. From 1999 to 2001, Embraer was Brazil's leading exporter, achieving a positive foreign exchange balance of $1.1 billion during that period. The company's controlling group, with 60 percent of the voting shares, is formed by one of Brazil's

Embraer
ended the 2001 fiscal year with the **best** financial results of its **history.**

A SkyWest EMB120 in flight

The EMBRAER 170, first in a new family of airliners developed specifically for the regional market, will debut in 2003.

biggest investment conglomerates, Cia Bozano, and the country's two largest pension funds, Previ and Sistel. Emerging from state ownership into entrepreneurship, Embraer's management team is centered on one goal: customer satisfaction.

To reach that end, in 1999 Embraer formed a strategic alliance with European aerospace companies Aerospatiale–Matra (now EADS), Dassault Aviation, Snecma and Thomason (now Thales), which jointly acquired 20 percent of Embraer's voting shares. The company also has embarked on a joint venture with Liebherr International of Germany to found Embraer-Liebherr Equipamentos do Brasil S.A. (ELEB), to create additional opportunities for the company's land gear and hydraulic components business.

As a result, Embraer ended the 2001 fiscal year with the best financial results of its history, recording gross revenues of $2,971,200 and net income of $468 million — 32.7 percent greater than the $352.6 million recorded the previous fiscal year. Not to be outdone by its competitors, in 2001 Embraer invested $128 million back into research and development of new products, and maintenance and improvement of existing products. An additional $106.1 million went toward enhancing the company's industrial capacity.

Closing 2001 with an impressive order backlog of $23.4 billion ($10.7 billion in firm orders and $12.7 billion in options), Embraer moved strongly into 2002, delivering 60 aircraft in the first six months.

Even with the worldwide economic slump, Embraer's cumulative net sales for the first six months of 2002 totaled $1.147 billion. Cumulative net income through June 30 came to $104.5

million, and the company invested a generous $76.6 million into R&D and maintaining and improving existing models.

After 33 years in the business of designing, manufacturing, selling and supporting aircraft for the world's commercial, defense and business markets, Embraer has experienced almost everything, but the company's symbiotic relationship with SkyWest stands out.

"Suppliers, vendors and folks trying to sell stuff are crawling all over each other to get the SkyWest contract, including manufacturers like Embraer," Reina says, "because Sky-West maintains a good product, always pays their bills and, from Embraer's standpoint, they're a fabulous airline to be associated with. But even more than that, they're there for us when we need them, like they were when they prefunded the engines and avionics in 1993. It is a huge deal to do that with an air fra-

The Embraer U.S.A headquarters, Fort Lauderdale, Florida

mer and signifies a level of trust we think is critical to the relationship. This is a perfect example of what we try to do: establish a relationship where we help each other, making sure the planes operate as they should, so they make money and we make money."

AVMAX GROUP, INC.

A world leader in aviation support and management services, Avmax Group Inc. is one of SkyWest's most recent partners. Established professionals, well-versed in the operations of modern corporate and airline industries, founded the Canadian company in 1996.

Avmax continues to grow, aggressively seeking additions to its 180-person team.

Shortly thereafter, SkyWest and Avmax struck up what was to become an excellent business relationship. In May 2002, the two signed a four-year contract for heavy maintenance and modification support at Avmax Group's Calgary facility.

With 75 percent of the company's business international, Calgary is home to the Avmax Group head office. An immense amount of aviation expertise exists in the area, and Calgary International Airport, accessible and well-known worldwide, adds strength to Avmax's position in the industry. Avmax is a partner in Airdrie Airpark, a 602-acre, privately owned development geared toward commercial aviation and related businesses, which is the only operation of its kind in Canada.

The Avmax Heavy Maintenance Center in Calgary, approved by Transport Canada, JAA and FAA for maintenance, provides full-service capabilities for corporate operators and regional airlines such as SkyWest. With its sister company, Western Avionics, the Center encompasses more than 60,000 square feet of hangar and support shop space. The hangars are strategically located to take advantage of the many subcontract support services offered in the area, including non-destructive testing, composite repairs, interior and exterior refinishing, engineering services, and engine propeller repair and overhaul.

Western Avionics, which merged with Avmax Group in 2002, represents all the major manufacturers of avionics and instruments. Services include new and used equipment sales, avionics service and instrument shop, equipment rental and exchanges, corporate/regional/commercial/charter installations, engineering certification, CAD, and transportable runway systems and navaids. The regional Western Avionics

office, located at the Vancouver International Airport, houses a state-of-the-art gyro overhaul and repair shop, avionics service, and an instrument shop. With the support of these facilities, Avmax inspects and repairs SkyWest aircraft, performs reconfigurations and modifications, and installs avionics and retrofits.

The Heavy Maintenance Center at Calgary also provides mobile repair parties to support manufacturers and operators throughout the world, offering many subcontract support services including repairs, modifications, airline start-up, and asset management.

Heavy Maintenance is only one division of Avmax Group, however. From locations in Calgary, Asia, Europe and the Middle East, the Aviation Division is committed to quality service in airline and corporate crewing, airline start-ups, aircraft management, and pilot and flight attendant training. Most crews have training capabilities on the aircraft and have been involved in course development. The division provides test flights, acceptance flights, ferry flights, simulator training, check flights and line flying for existing and start-up operators on many types of aircraft.

Avmax Group is also a worldwide leader in charter service, offering aircraft such as the

Heavy maintenance facility, Calgary

Aircraft delivery day

Learjet 60 and Challenger 604. The company's clientele, which includes individuals and corporations, demands privacy and the highest level of service achievable. Avmax Group crews meet this standard. They are professional and cordial, delivering to clients a turnkey solution to their travel requirements.

In partnership with Rheinland Air Services, Avmax Group delivers maintenance, avionics, training and management services in Europe. The partnership between these two proven companies provides an elite center in Central Europe delivering top-quality heavy maintenance to the marketplace with the knowledge, experience and inventory to service corporate and regional aircraft.

Calgary International Airport

Avmax Group has achieved such rapid success due to strong alliances with aircraft manufacturers and fellow aviation support companies and, most of all, because of its dedicated personnel. After the events of 9/11, Avmax, along with the rest of the aviation industry, was forced to make some drastic changes to remain viable. Unfortunately, that required several layoffs, but the remaining employees did what was needed to keep the company going.

Thanks to these dedicated employees and customers, it took only three months for Avmax Group to recover from the economic downturn. In January, the company was able to re-hire those who were affected by the layoffs. Today Avmax continues to grow, aggressively seeking additions to its 180-person team.

The Avmax team is headed by leaders who believe in forming strong business and personal relationships with partners such as SkyWest.

From corporate boardroom to airport tarmac, Avmax Group's business philosophy truly focuses on people, relationships and communication. The people at Avmax have created an environment that has attracted customers internationally. Relationships developed through Avmax have provided opportunities leading to significant growth and diversification for various support services within the aviation industry.

For example, in May 2002, Avmax brought together three countries and four companies with one common vision: to strive toward a world-class and internationally recognized training center in China for flight crew (both pilots and flight attendants), maintenance, management, and ground personnel. Communication sustains the Avmax environment, strengthens its relationships, and denotes Avmax as a leader in aviation management and support services.

Avmax customers appreciate the company's attention to detail, as well as its strict control over budgets and deadlines. Offering its clients a unique opportunity to obtain all their aviation requirements from a single source, Avmax helps them save time and money by eliminating the need for multiple sourcing.

Its new four-year contract with SkyWest is proof that, over the years, Avmax has provided the highest standard of professionalism, quality, and service in a cost-effective environment. Avmax Group's goal is to continue to meet or exceed this customer's expectations by ensuring high reliability for the SkyWest fleet long into the future.

John Binder	President
Don Parkin	Vice President, Operations
Rick Giacomuzzi	Vice President, Financing & CFO
Michael Zelenski	Vice-President, Aviation
Vince Scott	Vice President &GM, Western Avionics
Bob Williams	Vice President, Marketing and International Sales
Russ Binder	Director of Maintenance
Gary Graham	Director of Quality Assurance
Bob Waddell	Director of Administration
Davide Seneshen	Director of Aviation
Dave Rohee	Director of Aviation (Asia)
Len Burren	Controller, Western Avionics

BOMBARDIER AEROSPACE

The relationship between SkyWest Airlines and Bombardier Aerospace dates back to 1987, when the Regional Jet Division of Canadian aircraft manufacturer Canadair Ltd. began soliciting orders for its new and radical Canadair Regional Jet. The aircraft was radical because it was the first 50-seat jet airliner designed expressly for regional airlines such as SkyWest.

The project was greeted with great skepticism in the airline industry. At that time, regional airlines operated smaller piston engine and turboprop aircraft, and there was doubt that regional airlines could afford to take on jets, which cost more both to acquire and operate, and still make a profit.

Early vision. SkyWest was not among the skeptics, according to Eric McConachie. At the time, he led the Canadair Regional Jet marketing organization.

"Jerry Atkin signed a Memorandum of Understanding covering 10 CRJs in March, 1989 while it was still a paper airplane; the program had not even been officially launched," McConachie recalled. "We had flown Jerry and other SkyWest executives in one of our Canadair Challenger corporate jets, which was the baseline for the regional jet design. That helped to prove the concept of a regional jet to the SkyWest people and, I think, really heightened their interest."

SkyWest has ordered 100 CRJs

Thomas E. Appleton, who recently retired as President of the Bombardier Amphibious Aircraft Division, joined the Canadair Regional Jet marketing team in 1991 and played a major role in turning the Memorandum of Understanding into the firm order for 10 Canadair Regional Jets plus options for an additional 10. The contract was signed on August 17, 1993.

"Comair was the North American launch customer for the regional jet and began revenue service in June of 1993," Appleton said. "Jerry Atkin waited to see Comair's initial operating numbers, and when he saw them, he immediately called Montreal (where Canadair was located). He wanted the airplane. I was in Europe and immediately flew to New York where a Challenger picked me up and we continued to St. George for further negotiations."

(By this time, Canadair had been acquired from the Government of Canada by Bombardier, Inc., a Montreal-based manufacturer of snowmobiles, personal watercraft and railway transportation equipment. Bombardier later bought de Havilland Canada from the government and created Bombardier Aerospace. The corporation then merged the marketing, sales, contracts and customer support for the regional jet and de Havilland's Dash 8 turboprop airliners into a single unit, Bombardier Aerospace, Regional Aircraft. Its headquarters are at the former de Havilland facility in northwest Toronto, Ontario. Bombardier also acquired Learjet of Wichita, Kansas, and created Bombardier Aerospace, Business Aircraft to market the Challenger and Learjet lines of corporate jets.)

CRJ beat any competition. SkyWest had considered other aircraft before settling on the Canadian-built regional jet.

Applying final details to a CRJ

Flying for United Express

"When we first approached Delta about taking over some of their routes, it was obvious that we'd need a jet," Atkin said. "Once that was settled, timing was a factor and that narrowed the choice to three aircraft. Two of them were larger aircraft that would have put us too close in capacity to the Delta aircraft that we would be replacing. Second, their seat-mile costs were no better than the CRJ's, so there was no point in going to a larger aircraft."

SkyWest put its first regional jet into revenue service in March 1994. One month later, Atkin said, "I'm very satisfied with the Canadair Regional Jet. It is a very high quality, unique product that offers the right size of aircraft with jet speed, economy and comfort. That's never been done before."

Thus, SkyWest Airlines, because of its far-sighted management team, became one of the earliest players in what would become a revolutionary development in the airline industry, the astounding success of the regional jet.

It's an amazing story. Even in their most optimistic forecasts, the original marketing team thought they might sell 450 CRJs over a 20-year period. But, a little more than 10 years after the aircraft entered service, Bombardier has taken orders for more than 1,200, of which SkyWest Airlines has ordered 100 for routes operated for Delta Connection and United Express. Adding conditional orders and options, the CRJ program totals almost 2,500 aircraft, making it the most successful regional aircraft program in history.

"SkyWest, one of the early believers in the regional jet concept, undoubtedly contributed to the almost immediate success of the CRJ program," said John Giraudy, President of Bombardier Aerospace, Regional Aircraft. "SkyWest did much to prove the concept. Many airlines around the world witnessed what SkyWest and other airlines were doing with the aircraft, looked at the reliability and especially the profitability of the airplane, and came on board."

Success upon success. Successes tend to build upon themselves. What began as a single airplane model has grown into a family. Renamed the Bombardier CRJ Series a few years ago, the family now includes the 40- to 50-passenger CRJ200, 70-seat CRJ700 and 86-seat CRJ900.

Bombardier's regional aircraft family also includes three turboprop models. These are the 37- to 39-seat Q200, 50- to 56-seat Q300 and 68- to 78-seat Q400. The "Q" means Quiet. Bombardier Aerospace and Ultra Electronics of Cambridge, England, have developed a Noise and Vibration Suppression (NVS) system (originally designed to make nuclear submarines quieter). This makes the cabin of the propeller-driven aircraft almost as quiet and vibration free — in some cases more so — as a pure jet aircraft.

CRJ assembly plant, Montreal

Bombardier Aerospace, Regional Aircraft's mandate is to have the right aircraft available for regional airlines when they are required. The CRJ was such an aircraft, as were the Q200, Q300 and Q400. Developing the aircraft, and delivering them on schedule, has helped Bombardier Aerospace become the third-largest manufacturer of civil aircraft in the world, after Boeing of the United States and Airbus of Europe.

"We are very proud of our long-standing partnership with SkyWest Airlines," said Giraudy. "Our regional jet has done great things for them; their success with the airplane has been copied by airlines around the world, and that has helped with the success of the CRJ program."

SkyWest
did much
to prove the
regional
jet concept.

PARKER AEROSPACE

On May 1, 2002, Charles Lindbergh's grandson, Erik, followed in the aviation pioneer's footsteps by duplicating his grandfather's historic 1927 trans-Atlantic flight to Paris. Thanks to advances in the aerospace industry, Erik made the nonstop, solo run in about 17 hours (approximately half the time it took Charles). Although Erik's single-engine Lancair Columbia 300 and Charles' "Spirit of St. Louis" were vastly different machines in most ways, they had one thing in common: components manufactured by Parker. Even in the early days of aviation, the company's reputation for producing reliable hydraulic connectors led Charles Lindbergh to use Parker's leak-tight fuel fittings.

This reputation for quality, combined with decades of devotion to customer service, has made

the Aerospace Group of Parker Hannifin Corporation a leader in its industry. Today, major airliner manufacturers such as Embraer and Bombardier look to Parker Aerospace for design, manufacture and service of hydraulic, fuel and pneumatic components, systems and related electronic controls. With sales of more than $1 billion annually in aerospace and high-technology markets, Parker Aerospace strives to achieve its number one objective: providing premier customer service.

SkyWest Airlines is one of Parker's satisfied customers. Their relationship began in 1986. Parker designs, manufactures and supports major products for all the aircraft SkyWest flies. For example, on the Embraer EMB120, major Parker products include fuel valves, fuel pumps, flap actuators and electronic flap actuators. For the Canadair CRJ100/200, Parker provides fuel valves, fuel pumps, lubrication and scavenge pumps, and AC motor pumps. Looking toward the future, Parker's Abex Division is the hydraulic system designer, manufacturer and supplier for the brand-new Bombardier Continental Business Jet, BD100. There are more than 100 firm orders for this airplane, with first delivery scheduled for the end of 2002.

In the early days of the EMB120 program, SkyWest Vice-President of Maintenance Mike Gibson and Parker Aerospace's Customer Support Commercial Division worked very close, establishing some of the best maintenance and troubleshooting capabilities in existence today for the flight control and flap system. With the help of SkyWest Engine Programs Manager Dave Moran, Parker's Customer Support Commercial Division was able to enhance the EMB120 engine life through usage of Parker PW100 fuel nozzles. Numerous Parker advertisements in industry publications have featured SkyWest airplanes.

One high point in the SkyWest/Parker relationship occurred in 1991. SkyWest Manager of Aircraft Support Carolyn Poland and Director of Quality Steve Bovee stood up on behalf of Parker at the Embraer Worldwide Operators Conference and said that if any operators at the conference wanted to know what product support was all about, they needed to look at Parker's Customer Support Organization.

What lies behind such a commendation? Parker's flexible programs, which allow for customized support in cost per hour, extended warranties, guaranteed repair turnaround times, rotatable exchange programs, spares leasing, special salvages, level-payment plans, advance shipments, direct maintenance cost guarantee, flexible sustainment and performance-based

Parker Aerospace's Customer Support Commercial Division

> Parker Aerospace **strives** to achieve its number one objective: providing **premier** customer **service.**

Parker Aerospace Group headquarters located in Irvine, California

integrated logistics support. Parker creates customized programs in order to be SkyWest's best ally in achievement. Parker Aerospace provides SkyWest with premiere customer service, available anywhere in the world, any time of day or night. Parker Aerospace Customer Support Organization service centers are strategically located nationally in Arizona, California, Georgia, Massachusetts, Michigan, New York and Ohio, and internationally in Brazil, China, Germany, Japan, Malaysia and Singapore.

Building on and improving customer relationships, Parker has developed and is enhancing its online status-reporting capabilities for repairs, overhauls and spares. In today's uncertain economic climate, the aerospace industry is seeking to boost revenue and speed up time-consuming processes. Real-time collaboration between suppliers, customers and partners has become critical. Computer-aided integration of suppliers with customer order management systems, such as Parker Hannifin's PHConnect System, is one solution.

The PHConnect System, a Web-based portal, allows all Parker operating units to connect globally via an enterprise gateway so that customers and suppliers alike can deal with all 122 company divisions as though they were a single entity. Previously, customers had to place multiple orders to obtain products, receive invoices and conduct other types of business. Implementing the new global IT system has allowed them to place orders, check inventory availability, and review order and shipment status and billing information, as well as obtain basic and advanced information about products and services. The shift has freed the company from transactional and lower-level service responsibilities, and permitted Parker to focus on higher-level sales and customer service.

Parker also implements its complete supply chain goals by empowering suppliers to review manufacturing schedules, long-range product forecasts, accounts payable status, product drawings, PO status and quarterly ratings through PHConnect. Using this new information, suppliers lower their overall inventory and enter into long-term agreements with Parker that have service guarantees and price reductions. PHConnect information lets Parker analyze buying patterns, leverage supplier spending and develop better forecasts of customer demand. The result? Leaner, more efficient operation, and cost and time savings for customers such as SkyWest.

Parker's October 15, 2002, presentation to investors emphasized the strong outlook for regional jets. It also reiterated the company's commitment to be number one in the fundamentals of premiere customer service: delivering quality parts on time, providing value-added service, and creating and developing the best systems possible. SkyWest passengers will reap the benefits of Parker's success in these areas for years to come.

. . . .

With annual sales of $6 billion, Parker Hannifin Corporation is the world's leading diversified manufacturer of motion and control technologies, providing systematic, precision-engineered solutions for a wide variety of commercial, mobile, industrial and aerospace markets.

Parker Aerospace employs 5,200 people at operating plants and service offices worldwide, including facilities in Arizona, California, Georgia, Massachusetts, Michigan, New York, South Carolina, Ohio and Utah, and internationally in Brazil, China, England, France, Germany, Japan, Malaysia, Mexico and Singapore.

**Parker Aerospace
Customer Service Centers:**

Glendale, *Arizona*
Irvine, *California*
Dublin, *Georgia*
Ayer, *Massachusetts*
Kalamazoo, *Michigan*
Smithtown, *New York*
Forest, *Ohio*
Jacarei, *Brazil*
Beijing, *China*
Wiesbaden, *Germany*
Yokohama, *Japan*
Kuala Lumpur, *Malaysia*
Singapore

ST. GEORGE, UTAH

Winging into St. George on a SkyWest airliner over vermilion cliffs and verdant green golf courses, it's hard to imagine the slow, dusty trek hundreds of pioneer settlers made to get here in 1852. From this same fruitful valley, tucked into Utah's southwestern corner, the visionary Atkin family would commence pioneering in another arena—regional air service—some 120 years later.

When the Mormons entered the Salt Lake Valley in 1847, fleeing persecution in the Midwest, their leader, Brigham Young, resolved that the Latter-day Saints would be economically independent of the rest of the nation. Realizing people would need clothing as well as food, he encouraged experimental plantings of cotton in the valley, and later in the Santa Clara and Virgin River basins, located 300 miles south of Salt Lake City at a lower altitude.

Their initial success led to a call to Church members in 1861 to colonize the area. Their

Huntsman Games athlete

assignment was to "grow cotton" and to consider the Cotton Mission as important as a call to preach the gospel among the nations. The area's chief settlement, St. George, was named to honor the presiding Mormon elder, counselor to Brigham Young and "Father of the South," George Albert Smith, who had selected most of the Cotton Mission families. Many of the town's founders hailed from the Deep South, bringing with them another name to describe the area, "Utah's Dixie."

The valley's elevation and climate—2,880 feet above sea level; average rainfall 8.30 inches; climate ranging from 55 degrees on average in winter to above 100 degrees in summer—did indeed produce abundant crops—eventually. However, the early years proved difficult. Southern farmers understood cotton but not irrigation or alkali in sandy soil. They fought unending battles with the Virgin River. Their dams, built on quicksand bottoms, were washed out yearly, sometimes several times. Drought, grasshoppers and malaria plagued them. Cash was short and many early settlers left.

In 1863, the year St. George became the county seat of Washington County, the LDS Church began assisting the colonists by granting subsidies out of tithing resources to construct a tabernacle and a temple in St. George—early "public works" projects. The St. George LDS Tabernacle was completed in 1875. Meanwhile, in 1871, Utah's first LDS Temple was commenced. Its 140-foot steeple still serves as a town landmark. Work on the temple, which cost $800,000, put food on the tables of many families when poverty was severe. It was dedicated in 1877.

To mark the 50th anniversary of the settlement of St. George, Dixie Academy was constructed in 1911. The LDS Church operated it until 1933, when it became a two-year college within the state higher education system. In the 1960s, a new Dixie College campus opened across town. Vocational courses were added to the curriculum, among them aviation programs that have long trained students for SkyWest employment. The college remains a hub of St. George's cultural life.

Since the 1960s, that culture has expanded to include a growing number of retirees and "snow-

Coral Canyon Golf Course

Dixie Center in St. George, Utah

birds," the latter comprising about a quarter of the winter population of 52,000. Brigham Young himself spent winters in St. George toward the end of his life. Completed in 1873, his home has been restored, filled with 19th-century furnishings and opened to tours. Tourism and recreation have become primary industries for St. George, diversifying Washington County's economic base beyond agriculture.

People of all ages recreate in countless ways in or around St. George. Nearly 30 miles of scenic walking, skating and biking paths weave through the area, connecting 22 neighborhood parks, streamside corridors, picturesque desertscapes and the historic town center. Just 45 minutes east lies breathtaking Zion National Park, now a rock climbing and, yes, skydiving destination. Seven miles north of St. George, Snow Canyon State Park offers camping, hiking, rock climbing and mountain biking year-round. "Snow" refers to Lorenzo and Erastus Snow, prominent pioneer leaders, not to the winter precipitation on the sunny, red rock marvels of this park, one of the area's best kept secrets and a photographer's dream.

With four courses to choose from, golfers need not set foot outside of town to enjoy their sport any day of the year. However, another seven are sprinkled along the surrounding "Red Rock Corridor," as *Golf Magazine* calls the area. The matchless views from nearly every hole make golf Washington County's #1 tourist attraction.

Scenery also has a lot to do with the popularity of the annual St. George Marathon, the 15th largest in the country. Rated in the Top 10 Most

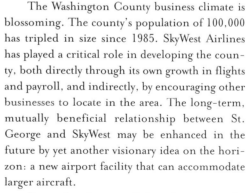
Sunbrook Golf Club
COURTESY ST. GEORGE AREA CVB · BRYCE THATCHER

Scenic Races by *Runner's World*. In 2002 it attracted 6,200 runners. Another annual event, the Huntsman Senior Games, brings international athletes over age 50 to St. George to compete in tennis, golf, horseshoes, biking, softball and basketball events. It is named for Jon M. Huntsman, head of Salt Lake City-based Huntsman Chemical Corporation (HCC), the largest privately held chemical company in the nation. Not to be outdone, ball players flock to The Canyons Softball Complex, where 38 acres of ball fields and concession buildings nestle in a setting surrounded by red rock vistas. Named the top softball complex in the country for the last four years by the National Softball Association, The Canyons hosts more than 100 tournaments annually.

The Washington County business climate is blossoming. The county's population of 100,000 has tripled in size since 1985. SkyWest Airlines has played a critical role in developing the county, both directly through its own growth in flights and payroll, and indirectly, by encouraging other businesses to locate in the area. The long-term, mutually beneficial relationship between St. George and SkyWest may be enhanced in the future by yet another visionary idea on the horizon: a new airport facility that can accommodate larger aircraft.

From the dreams of the pioneers to the drawing boards of their great-great-grandchildren, St. George and Washington County have offered fertile ground for the creative impulse — an urge shared by SkyWest Airlines, equally rooted in this red, red soil.

Matchless **views** from nearly every hole make **golf** Washington County's #1 tourist attraction.

STANDARD AERO

Standard Aero is high on customer service.

Building a long-term partnership is very important to both Standard Aero and SkyWest. Beginning in 1995, a complete assessment of the airline's engine maintenance and support needs was carried out. Since then, all through SkyWest's dynamic company growth and success, SkyWest and Standard Aero have worked closely together to achieve a single goal: to maintain the highest level of quality and service in order to make SkyWest's business more profitable.

An important part of the process has been the innovative TEAM™ (Total Engine Asset Management) approach developed by Standard Aero. The TEAM™ program targets the reduction of direct operating costs and the continuous improvement of quality and reliability.

Standard Aero is high on customer service. The company stations a highly skilled, full-time Engine Program Manager at SkyWest's main maintenance site in Salt Lake City, Utah. His sole responsibility is to assist in managing the technical maintenance, logistic and repair schedules for more than 300 engines, including the auxiliary power units that provide air conditioning, electricity and other internal power functions for SkyWest's fleet. Standard Aero's dedicated Program Manager stays in constant communication with Standard Aero repair facilities in Knoxville, Tennessee, Winnipeg, Canada, and Tilburg, The Netherlands. So at any given moment, he knows the status of the engines and what is being done to keep them flying safely.

In the ever-changing airline industry, Standard Aero understands the needs and requirements associated with owning, operating and maintaining an airline fleet. With repair facilities strategically located in Canada, the United States, Europe, Mexico, Australia and Asia, Standard Aero has earned a reputation for excellence through years of superior performance and customer satisfaction. Standard Aero's "rapid response" customer support team is available 24/7, providing emergency and troubleshooting support whenever and wherever customers need it.

Working together, SkyWest and the Standard Aero team provide valued SkyWest customers with a safe and enjoyable flight wherever the destination.

....

STANDARD AERO, A MEMBER OF DUNLOP STANDARD AEROSPACE GROUP, IS ONE OF THE WORLD'S LARGEST INDEPENDENT SMALL GAS TURBINE ENGINE AND ACCESSORIES REPAIR AND OVERHAUL COMPANIES. WITH OPERATIONS AROUND THE GLOBE, THE COMPANY PROVIDES A UNIQUE MIX OF MANAGEMENT AND MAINTENANCE REPAIR AND OVERHAUL SERVICES TO AIRLINE, BUSINESS AVIATION, HELICOPTER, GOVERNMENT/MILITARY AIRCRAFT AND INDUSTRIAL OPERATORS.

STANDARD AERO

Replacing parts on CF34 engine

Quality inspection of CF34 engine

FIELD AVIATION

From modest beginnings in 1947 in a small hangar in Oshawa, Ontario, providing maintenance support services to early airborne mapping activities across Canada, to currently employing over 500 dedicated individuals representing all major disciplines of aircraft maintenance, sales, modification, and manufacturing, Field Aviation has grown into a worldwide airline support center serving civilian and military markets.

Field Aviation provides a wide range of comprehensive maintenance services on all types

Field Aviation hangar, Calgary

of regional aircraft at facilities in Calgary and Toronto. Field has capabilities for heavy maintenance inspections, mobile repair parties, modifications, structural repairs, interior and exterior refinishing, and avionics work.

In the area of aircraft repair, maintenance, modifications and conversions, Field Aviation is an undisputed leader. Over 50 years of experience and a highly trained and talented team of aviation employees can solve any aircraft problem. Field Aviation is a true one-stop-shop.

From a basic machine shop supporting the Repair and Overhaul Division, Field's Manufacturing Center developed the expertise and capabilities to fabricate specialty parts to support its maintenance repair and overhaul business. Today, Field Aviation-Manufacturing and its alliance partners supply complete customer support for the de Havilland DHC-5 Buffalo and DHC-4 Caribou aircraft under license from Bombardier. Field also maintains a 24-hour customer service line. Using this service, a customer can order new parts, have components overhauled or exchanged, or obtain technical assistance from the Field Aviation Maintenance Repair and Overhaul Division at any time, as needs demand.

Members of the Field Aviation Engineering Group blend the knowledge gained from a dedicated team of technicians to develop product improvements through Supplemental Type Certificates to replacement parts via Parts Design Authority (Transport Canada's version of Parts Manufacturing Authority). Whether the requirement is to incorporate an Enhanced Ground Proximity Warning System or develop a Maritime Patrol aircraft equipped with the latest radar and surveillance equipment, Field has a solution to fit every customer's needs.

Field Aviation knows airplanes and has been demonstrating it for over 50 years. From the big to the small, Field serves customers worldwide, from supporting search-and-rescue aircraft with the Canadian Department of National Defense or Maritime Patrol aircraft in Australia, to working with SkyWest Airlines' Maintenance Team to ensure each aircraft is maintained to the highest standard.

The dynamic team at Field Aviation continues its proven track record of success, meeting and exceeding customer expectations. In partnering with SkyWest Airlines, Field has demonstrated the capability, flexibility, and strong skills to adapt to rapid technological change. Whether supporting various charities through the Sky-West-sponsored Mini Grand Prix car race in St. George, Utah, or developing modifications such as cockpit door protective devices to improve SkyWest passenger comfort or safety, Field Aviation and SkyWest will be working together to ensure customer satisfaction in the future.

> Field Aviation
> is a true
> **one-stop
> shop.**

1952 - 2002

50

FIELD CALGARY

BOISE AIRPORT CITY OF BOISE

In the 1990s, Idaho's Treasure Valley blossomed as the seventh-fastest-growing of the nation's 280 metropolitan areas. No wonder the Boise Airport, built in 1936 and most recently expanded in 1995, began to feel the crunch. As the volume of passenger traffic came to exceed capacity, administrators took steps to bring the facility into the 21st century. SkyWest Airlines has fully participated in this remarkable growth, having served southwestern Idaho and eastern Oregon travelers through this airport since 1988.

Construction is now under way. Boise Airport patrons soon will enjoy the first fruits of a long-term expansion program needed to accommodate growing passenger traffic — 3 million passengers annually, up an average 7.75 percent a year from 1998 to 2000 — as well as anticipated new carriers. The program focuses on a new 364,305-square-foot terminal, more than a third larger than the existing building.

The future of the Boise Airport

Phase 1, scheduled for completion in early 2003, consists of a new ticket lobby, baggage claim, pre-security retail shops, pre-security food and beverage area, rental car lobby, conference center and administrative offices. The second phase, housing a new security checkpoint, food court and ground-loading concourse, is expected to open in early 2004. Concourse B of the current terminal will remain, but administrators foresee the need for a new Concourse A, duplicate ticket and baggage lobbies, and additional parking in the near future.

Why Boise? Why not? Once the butt of stand-up comic routines, Boise has come into its own as a center for high-tech manufacturing and R&D, year-round outdoor recreation and a relaxed yet urban lifestyle.

The cultural hub for the Treasure Valley's 403,000 residents, Boise boasts its own philharmonic orchestra, opera, ballet and numerous professional and amateur theater companies. In summer, the world-class Idaho Shakespeare Festival delivers the words of the Bard to thousands; in fall, Boise State University's WAC football Broncos hit the blue turf; in winter, the Idaho Steelheads (one of Boise's three professional athletic teams) pump fans' adrenaline; in spring, the Boise River Festival and Gene Harris Jazz Festival attract big-name entertainers. Cultural facilities abound, including the World Center for Birds of Prey, Boise Art Museum, Idaho Historical Museum, Log Cabin Literary Center, Idaho Black History Museum, World Sports Humanitarian Hall of Fame, and the latest addition, dedicated in August 2002, the $1.5 million Idaho Anne Frank Human Rights Memorial.

Beyond Boise, the backcountry beckons. Countless river runners, backpackers, skiers, hunters and anglers begin their adventures at a Boise Airport arrival gate. SkyWest currently provides service to Boise Airport as Delta Connection and United Express. Its economical Embraer-120 turboprops and Canadair Regional Jets give these national carriers more frequent direct connections between Boise, Salt Lake City and San Francisco. Frequent flights also benefit travelers honing in on the Treasure Valley's Fortune 500 corporations, entrepreneurial start-ups, financial institutions and diverse array of manufacturing and service industries.

Even without much competition for passengers, Boise Airport obviously strives for excellence — one more advantage of this 21st-century city that still manages to feel a little like everyone's hometown.

Patrons will soon **enjoy** the first fruits of a long-term expansion **program.**

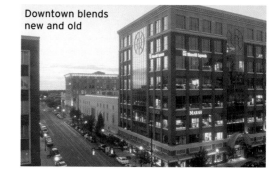

Downtown blends new and old

FRESNO YOSEMITE
INTERNATIONAL AIRPORT

Fresno County, with a quickly growing population 764,800, is an emerging metropolitan center with a rich cultural mix of more than 90 different nationalities. Fresno city has all the urban amenities (from a world-class opera company to a AAA baseball team) combined with the neighborly qualities of a small, familiar community.

Air travel has long been part of Fresno. The airport first began as an unpaved landing strip in a grain field belonging to State Senator

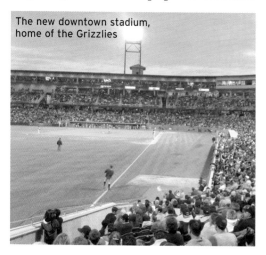
The new downtown stadium, home of the Grizzlies

W.F. Chandler and his family. In 1928, recognizing the need for a permanent aviation facility to serve the community, the Chandler family deeded their airfield and some 80 acres of land to the city, creating Fresno-Chandler Airport.

Commercial airline service began there in 1942, but moved to Hammer Field in 1946, making use of the old WWII facility. The new airport was designated Fresno Air Terminal (granting the airport the unique identifier "FAT" used today). SkyWest Airlines began flying to Fresno in 1985 as the SkyWest/Delta Connection. Ten years later, SkyWest/Continental Connection flights began. Today, SkyWest provides the majority of flights from FAT as United Express and Delta Connection service.

The facility changed its name to Fresno Yosemite International Airport in 1996 to better define its location. Fresno is the only city in the United States with three national parks in

its backyard: Kings Canyon, Sequoia and Yosemite. Winter and summer, they attract recreationists from around the world. Yosemite alone boasts nearly 350 miles of skiable trails and roads. The Merced and Tuolumne rivers sweep whitewater paddlers down miles of Class IV and Class V rapids. Day hikers follow in the steps of renowned naturalist and photographer Ansel Adams. Three national forests, scenic Sierra lakes and the Pacific Ocean offer easy day trips for family fun.

Closer to home, springtime visitors can follow the beautiful Blossom Trail through nearby San Joaquin Valley communities to savor fruit trees alive with fragrance and bursting with colorful blooms. The largest agricultural farm equipment show in the world, the World Ag Expo, takes place every February in Tulare, attracting farmers, ranchers and entrepreneurs from China to Australia.

Known as "California Without the Cost," Fresno offers affordable housing and excellent schools, including prestigious institutions such as California State University, Fresno. At the heart of this busy and growing state, Fresno Yosemite International (FYI) is the premier airport, furnished with a sophisticated Category IIIb instrument landing system that allows aircraft operation even in the valley's winter tule fog.

Strengthening relationships with carriers, growing the passenger base to the San Joaquin Valley, and developing a strong regional jet maintenance hub for SkyWest are FYI's long-range goals as it works with its aviation and airline partners in a highly competitive industry.

A sophisticated Category IIIb instrument **landing system** allows aircraft operation even in the valley's winter tule fog.

Yosemite

MONTEREY PENINSULA
AIRPORT DISTRICT

At Monterey Bay, the Pacific Ocean takes a big bite out of Central California. Long an inspiration to artists, the spectacular beauty of Monterey County's 99-mile coastline between Los Angeles and San Francisco is matched by the fertile productivity of the Salinas Valley just inland. Here, writer John Steinbeck was born 100 years ago. Within the county's confines he set some of his most popular novels: *Cannery Row, East of Eden, Of Mice and Men* and *The Grapes of Wrath.*

In 1940, *The Grapes of Wrath* won the Pulitzer Prize. Just a year later, Senate Bill No. 1300 authorized the creation of the Monterey Peninsula Airport District. The country was still recovering from the Depression and about to enter World War II.

Airport runways and a hangar had been built in 1937, five years after Samuel Morse leased 37 acres for an airport to promote tourism for the Del Monte Hotel. Almost continually from 1939 on, United Airlines served the airport's passenger and freight customers. In 1987, SkyWest's relationship with the Airport District began, first as a contractor for both United and Delta Airlines and, most recently as United Express.

Monterey Peninsula Airport is the gateway to one of America's most beautiful getaways, from the majesty of Big Sur rising abruptly above the breakers to the verdant fields stretching 50 miles from Salinas past King City. This "Salad Bowl of the Nation" produces more than $2.5 billion worth of fresh fruits and vegetables annually, making agriculture Monterey County's largest industry.

Tourism isn't far behind. History buffs walk Monterey's Path of History or visit the $11 million Steinbeck Center in Old Town Salinas. Lovers are pampered at spas and B&Bs; shoppers flock to upscale stores in Carmel, Outlets at Pacific Grove and dozens of small local shops where treasures await discovery. The venerable Monterey Jazz Festival attracts hundreds of stellar performers and thousands of music lovers each September.

Some 65,000 divers a year from around the world drop into the deeps of Monterey Bay Sanctuary, lured by the kelp forest's unique beauty, good visibility and safe conditions. This underwater canyon has been dubbed the best beach dive in the United States by *Scuba Diving* magazine. Landlubbers hike the rocky shoreline from one breathtaking vista and fascinating tide pool to another, or observe marine plants and animals at the world-famous Monterey Bay Aquarium.

Golf Digest recently named Monterey County the world's #1 golf destination. A round at legendary Pebble Beach Golf Links (just $2 for gentlemen and $1.50 for ladies when John Steinbeck was 17 years old) costs $300-plus per person, but 24 other golf courses offer a host of options to more budget-minded duffers.

Ever since Franciscan Friars planted wine grapes near Soledad Mission 200 years ago, the county's climate has produced intensely flavored fruit. Today, 40 wineries operate in Monterey County, from giants Robert Mondavi and E.J. Gallo to boutiques like Paraiso Springs, Smith & Hook and Scheid Vineyards — a growing industry that would have pleased the *The Grapes of Wrath's* author no end.

Landlubbers hike the rocky shoreline from one **breathtaking** *vista to another.*

Monterey Bay sunrise

IMAGE COURTESY OF MONTEREY COUNTY CONVENTION AND VISITORS BUREAU

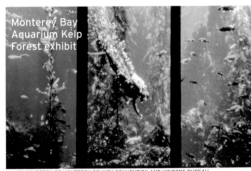

Monterey Bay Aquarium Kelp Forest exhibit

IMAGE COURTESY OF MONTEREY COUNTY CONVENTION AND VISITORS BUREAU

WALKER FIELD AIRPORT

W alker Field, strategically located at Grand Junction in the "banana belt" of western Colorado, serves a diverse mix of commercial and general aviation, federal government and air cargo clients. Thanks to state-of-the-art navigation and landing aids and

the mild Grand Valley climate, Walker Field has been closed due to weather only 28 hours in the last 25 years—a record few airports can match, especially those just two hours or less from world-class ski resorts (Aspen, Vail and Telluride) and national parks (Arches and Canyonlands).

"We consider Grand Junction not only a regional airport for western Colorado, but include eastern Utah as part of our 'happy family,'" explains Corinne Nystrom, Walker Field Airport manager. "Lots of people from outside the U.S.A., who have done the New York/D.C.

Optimum weather conditions

routine and are looking for the Wild West, come to Canyonlands."

The current $3 million, multi-year renovation of Walker Field's 20-year-old terminal building will add two passenger loading bridges — a first for any western Colorado airport. The improvements are intended to give passengers a smoother, more efficient and enjoyable experience.

Walker Field rebounded quickly from the effects of 9/11. Passenger traffic remained constant, and annual operations and revenues increased. "Although the national average shows emplanements about 9 percent below a year ago, people actually use this airport more than they did before 9/11," Nystrom notes. "They're saying 'We're not going to let 9/11 stop us from doing what we want to do.'"

In addition to tourism, which accounts for 70 percent of its travelers, cargo is vital for Walker Field. After Federal Express initiated direct operations to Grand Junction from Memphis in 1998, air freight and cargo traffic grew rapidly. The Airport Authority's long-range plan envisions a new multi-user cargo facility to give haulers more space to work and enough ramp to accommodate more cargo and passenger flights.

As an Airport Authority, Walker is a self-governing entity independent of local government control. The Board of Commissioners, which oversees the Authority as well as the staff, can make decisions right on the spot instead of taking them to city hall or the county courthouse. "It makes for a more efficient operation, which is ultimately good for the airlines," Nystrom says.

One airline that benefits from this efficiency is SkyWest, which began flying into Walker Field in 1983, just 11 years after SkyWest began, and 55 years after Grand Junction *Daily Sentinel* publisher, Walter Walker, led residents in establishing the community's first public airport.

"We have seen SkyWest evolve as an airline," Nystrom says. "They started with Metroliners, then upgraded to Brasilias. Now we have a regional jet coming in every day, too. It's a very popular flight in the morning, almost always full.

"SkyWest plays a huge role at this airport because they are not only our Delta Connection carrier to Salt Lake City but our United Express carrier to Denver," Nystrom says. "SkyWest carries basically two-thirds of our commercial traffic. They are efficient, courteous and friendly, their on-time performance is really good, and their safety record is outstanding. They're a wonderful airline and we love them!"

Walker Field
rebounded
quickly
from the
effects
of 9/11.

Gateway to western Colorado

CEDAR CITY, UTAH

As one of SkyWest's original destinations, Cedar City provides a prolific history and a visionary future joined with year-round excitement, astonishing beauty, and unbeatable outdoor recreation. Often called the Gateway to the National Parks, Cedar is centrally located within an hour-and-a-half drive of Zion National Park, Bryce Canyon National Park, and Cedar Breaks National Monument. Many enjoy rock climbing, mountain biking and golfing as well as snowboarding and skiing at Brian Head Resort, the Tony Award-winning Utah Shakespearean Festival and the Utah Summer Games. Cedar is home to Southern Utah University and, with its business-friendly environment, boasts several nationally recognized industrial businesses.

Bryce Canyon, located near Cedar City, Utah.

IC GROUP

IC Group, like Skywest, had its beginnings in a small Utah town. Today, IC Group has over 65,000 square feet of manufacturing facilities, 250 employees, and sales people across the United States. The IC Group products and services include specialized secure check and forms printing, full-color commercial printing, electronic print and mail services and highly customized online ordering for our customers. We continue to expand our products, services, equipment and facilities to better serve our clients and meet the ever-increasing demands of technology. Make IC Group your premier provider for all your business printing needs.

IC Group / SkyWest Airlines—A Great Partnership

FUTURE AVIATION, INC.

Future Aviation of Fort Myers, Florida was established in 1984. We are a FAA/JAA approved accessory Class I, II, III repair facility (XC4R643M) specializing in the repair and overhaul of starter generators, electrical parts, GCUs, fans, hydraulics, wheels and brakes. FAI has been the #1 TRW/Lucas repair station worldwide since 1991. Other authorizations include Embraer, Saab, Hartman Electrical and KGS Electronics. We are proud of our long-standing association with SkyWest and our commitment to provide exceptional quality, competitive pricing and the best turn times in the industry.

Congratulations, SkyWest, on Your 30-Year Anniversary!
Best Wishes for Your Continued Success!

Future Aviation facility located in Fort Myers, Florida.

AAR LANDING GEAR SERVICES

Founded in 1951 as a surplus parts company, AAR has grown into a global aviation aftermarket support company, providing inventory and logistics services, maintenance, repair and overhaul, manufacturing and aircraft and engine sales and leasing to over 13,000 customers. Over the years, AAR has established a reputation for delivering what it promises, serving commercial, military and general aviation customers. AAR's philosophy is to focus on strong customer relationships by delivering performance guarantees, low costs, high availability, short turn-times and personalized service.

AAR Landing Gear Services, located in Miami, Florida, specializes in the maintenance, repair, overhaul and exchange of landing gear for aircraft of all types. With the acquisition of Tempco Hydraulics in 1999, AAR LGS' capabilities expanded to providing comprehensive service to regional carriers and enabled us to support SkyWest Airlines and their fleet of EMB120 and CRJ aircraft. AAR helps customers profit and prosper by building, enhancing and protecting their aviation assets.

EMB120 nose gear

AAR LGS' main commitment is their clients, and they build AAR LGS' relationships using small touches while concentrating on big issues. Customers needs are individual, and AAR LGS' goal is to find ways to meet their requirements anywhere, anytime. Their specialized "Tiger Teams" are available for travel to customer sites. The teams can repair and overhaul landing gears and related components, as well as wheel and brake systems. This on-site ability to service aircraft reduces the downtime for customers.

AAR LGS operates under the AAR motto of "AAR Total Solutions". AAR LGS is proud of their ability to perform all phases of the overhaul process of landing gears in house. Among their capabilities are Stress Relief, NDT Inspections, grinding, machining, polishing, and plating. Additional services would include wheels and brakes, exchange programs, and manufacturing.

Components are run through the shop using a computerized Inspection Condition Report System, designed and developed by AAR LGS' team of engineers and computer programmers. It's the only system in existence and it gives the customer a complete history of the work performed. The team of certified engineers oversees all aspects of the overhaul process, and when required, creates solutions for not so common situations that may arise during the overhaul process.

AAR Landing Gear Services meets the definition of quality and customer satisfaction that AAR Corporation is known for. AAR LGS' strength is in their people. They're knowledgeable and responsive experts who care about customer success in measurably different ways. AAR's goal is to give their customers a competitive advantage.

AAR LGS has been able to eliminate the inconsistency normally associated with a service organization by providing high quality workmanship on each of the components they service. Because of AAR LGS' unique processing systems, they are able to deliver consistent quality in the services provided.

AAR LGS will continue to operate and grow by providing the best service at the best value to their customers. AAR finds a way, every day, to use speed, strength, integrity, ingenuity, obsession with quality, and relentless pursuit of opportunities to enhance customers' success.

CRJ nose gear

> AAR LGS will **continue** to operate and **grow** by providing the **best** service at the best **value** to their customers.

EUGENE AIRPORT

The Eugene Airport is the second busiest airport in the state of Oregon.

In 1919, local businessman and chairman of the Eugene Chamber of Commerce Aviation Committee Mahlon Sweet persuaded the people of Eugene to assist him in establishing the Eugene Air Park, Eugene's first municipal airport and the first municipally owned airport on the west coast.

By 1939, Sweet had successfully campaigned to have a larger, more modern airport constructed for the city of Eugene. May 1, 1943, Mahlon Sweet Field was dedicated. Today, Mahlon Sweet Field, now known as the Eugene Airport, is the second busiest airport in the State of Oregon and the fifth largest airport in the Pacific Northwest.

SAN DIEGO INTERNATIONAL AIRPORT

Congratulations to SkyWest for 30 great years! San Diego International Airport celebrates its own 75th anniversary in 2003 as we also honor the centennial of flight. As the region's only major commercial service airport, it contributes $4.5 billion annually to our regional economy, $1.8 billion in personal income and 4 percent of the region's total economic output. Every job at San Diego International Airport contributes to another 15 jobs in the region. And, as air travel continues to evolve, and San Diego remains one of the busiest air transportation centers of our kind, we look forward to working hand-in-hand with SkyWest to continue to deliver world-class service to our customers.

OXNARD AIRPORT

Oxnard has become one of California's best kept secrets.

Since 1946 travelers have used Oxnard Airport as a gateway to beautiful Ventura County, California. The reasons to visit or live in Ventura County are as varied as the wide range of amenities it offers. From business, technology and education to recreation and quality living, the "Gold Coast" contains the very best Southern California has to offer. Beginning with DC-3 service in the late 1940s and continuing today with SkyWest service, Oxnard Airport continues to meet the challenges brought about by the changes in air transportation and is a viable option for tomorrow's travelers in Ventura County.

COACH'S OATS

It started in the kitchen of Lynn and Bonnie Rogers' small condominium. They ground raw oats and cooked them into hot oatmeal that wowed everyone who tasted it. Lynn was a college gymnastics coach so the recipe soon became known as "Coach's Oats." Ten years later, Coach's Oats is a thriving, family-run business with oatmeal, energy bars, cookies and other good stuff. "Our signature products match up perfectly with SkyWest's signature service," Rogers said. " The support of the great people at SkyWest has made a real difference in the lives of our employees. Thank you for the opportunity to play a small role in your well-deserved success."

Coach's Oats products are a favorite among SkyWest's inflight crew and passengers alike.

HOT SECTION TECHNOLOGIES

HOT SECTION TECHNOLOGIES, INC.
FAA APPROVED REPAIR STATION NO. YV2R333L

Hot Section Technologies, Inc. (HST) was founded in 1986 and is located in Santa Paula, California. The company specializes in the repair, overhaul and modification of non-rotating turbine engine and airframe parts. HST is an approved General Electric, Honeywell and Pratt & Whitney Canada repair station. The company provides its customers with an exciting, cost-effective option to escalating maintenance costs. SkyWest Airlines was one of HST's first customers and their continued support has been a key factor in HST's successes.

PEERLESS COFFEE

Founded in 1924 by John Vukasin, Peerless Coffee Company is one of the premier, family owned and operated gourmet coffee roasters on the west coast. For over 78 years, we have combined a tradition of quality with excellence and have mastered the art of roasting and blending the finest Arabica coffees to perfection! Voted #1 roaster by the *San Francisco Chronicle*, Peerless is committed to quality, service, sustainability, and community and is a proven leader in the Specialty Coffee Industry. We salute SkyWest on their 30th year of service and share their commitment to excellence!

"I've never tried to **predict** what's going to happen in the **future.**
I do know that no matter how the world changes, a quality **vision** and
the ability to **adapt** will help us react in the best possible way."

— JERRY ATKIN